How the Golden Age

of Television Turned

How the Golden Age

of Television Turned
My Hair to Silver

Kenneth Whelan

WALKER AND COMPANY • NEW YORK

First published in the United States of America
in 1973 by the Walker Publishing Company, Inc.

Published simultaneously in Canada
by Fitzhenry & Whiteside, Limited, Toronto

ISBN: 0-8027-0420-4

Library of Congress Catalog Card Number: 73-87273

Printed in the United States of America.

10 9 8 7 6 5 4 3 2 1

Contents

How the Golden Age of Television Turned My Hair to Silver

Foreword

I can't remember ever wanting to be a television director. I mean, I didn't go looking for it. The whole thing was sort of an accident. Fortunately, after twenty thousand dollars worth of psychiatry, I have completely recovered from that accident and now function with a certain degree of normalcy.

Up until that day in 1950 when I entered television through the back door, my career had been in legitimate show business. I was a dancer and choreographer by trade. Tap dancing was my specialty—an ancient art form very popular with the lower classes prior to World War II. Most people think I'm trying to be funny when I mention my former profession. If you ever want to get a laugh at a party, just mention that you once made your living growing mushrooms, robbing banks, or tap dancing.

Before the army interrupted things, I appeared in several Broadway musicals: "Louisiana Purchase," "By Jupiter," "My Dear Public," and "The Lady Comes Across." In "By Jupiter," I understudied Ray Bolger, who turned out to be the healthiest musical comedy star I've ever encountered. I was the choreographer in "My Dear Public," and the show turned out to be the biggest flop of the season. I was a chorus boy in the other two shows.

After World War II, the demand for tap dancers began to diminish. I continued to scratch out a meager existence at my trade for a few years, but by 1950 I was an unemployed tap dancer with a wife and two children. It was at this low point that a certain old female relative got me a job in television. I don't know how she did it, and I never wanted to know, but I think her influence was based on an illicit love affair with a United States senator in 1923. I wasn't terribly interested in television but I accepted the favor, figuring it would provide temporary employment until tap dancing came back in vogue.

The revival of "No, No, Nanette" in 1971, which brought tap dancing back to the world, proves that I should have waited.

CHAPTER 1

Sneaking In

I started out in television as an associate director, which is a pretty good place to start. It certainly suggested that my old female relative must have had a damn good illicit love affair with that United States senator.

The gentleman who handled my job interview was a credit to CBS. He was a WASP with warmth. He offered me coffee, and a cheese danish. "What sort of position did you have in mind, Mr. Whelan?"

"Oh, anything at all, sir. . . . I was thinking along the lines of a night watchman, or possibly a mimeograph operator. . . . You see, it's just temporary. I'm a tap dancer by trade."

3

"Come, come, Mr. Whelan. It would be a waste of nepotism and political pull to give you a job as a night watchman." He cut my cheese danish for me, then he continued. "I've been giving this a great deal of thought, and have decided to start you off as an associate director."

"That's nice. Are you sure I can handle it?"

"No problem."

That's how I got into television. And it's true.

CHAPTER **2**

First
Blooding

My first three weeks at CBS were called my "Observation Period." My only duties were to observe what was going on in the various studios, control rooms, film projection rooms, master control rooms, film editing rooms, scenic designing rooms, and any other rooms I might stumble into. At the end of these three weeks I was supposed to understand how a TV show was put on the air. I asked hundreds of people hundreds of questions, and at the end of my observation period I had a vague idea of what it was all about.

On my second day at CBS I was assigned to observe a local cooking show. My instructions were to watch the as-

5

sociate director, and try to get an idea of how he functioned. It was explained to me that this cooking show was an extremely simple production, and would be an easy way to break in. The day turned out to be a disaster. Remember, this was my second day of observing, and I was a raw virgin. My first day of observing had been wasted, watching the CBS personnel department fall apart completely. They had a lot of trouble accepting "ex-tap dancer" as a suitable background for associate director.

In order to understand the cooking show disaster, I have to supply you with a little information about the technical side of early television. Unfortunately, this little information was more than *I* possessed on my second day of observation.

In 1950, CBS had their own special name for their film projection room. They called it "Telecine" (pronounced Tela-ceenee). The projection room was, and is, the room where all motion picture film is sent out over the air. It is simply a large room filled with motion picture projectors. At that time each projector was set up in tandem with a "Telop" machine—CBS's name for their version of a slide projector. All of these projectors were hitched up to a small television camera by a . system of mirrors, and the whole unit was called a film chain. Again, I mention the fact that I knew nothing about projection rooms when I was assigned to observe this cooking show.

It was the first time I had ever been in a television control room, and I remember that I got a slight headache from the smell of the electronic equipment. It's hard to describe this smell, but if you stick your nose into the back of your television set after it's been running for an hour, you'll get the idea.

I stood quietly in the back of the control room and concentrated on observing. The people in the control room were preparing to go on the air, and their activities were a complete mystery to me. The only thing I learned in that first half hour was not to leave my empty coffee containers on the control room console.

About five minutes before air time, the man who was acting like a boss let out a yell. "Where's the AD? Who's the AD on this goddamn thing?" No one had an answer, so he grabbed a phone and furiously dialed a number. "Hello, schedule? . . . Peggy? . . . This is Vern. . . . Look, who did you assign to AD the cooking show? Nobody showed up. . . . Oh, fine! . . . Yeah, I know you're sorry, but this is the second time in two weeks you forgot to assign somebody!" He was angry, and, as he slammed the phone down, he spotted me standing at the back of the control room.

"Who are you?"

"I'm observing."

"I can see *that!* Who are you?"

My electronic headache became worse. "My name is Ken Whelan . . . and I'm going to be an associate director . . . and I'm observing what an associate director does."

"Well, you're wasting your time . . . I don't have an associate director! Come back some other day!"

He glanced at the clock. Then back to me. Suddenly, a fiendish smile appeared on his face. Later on, I realized that it was just a smile, but at the moment, it was a fiendish smile.

"Wait a minute! I've got a great idea, Len . . . ."

"Ken."

"Right, Ken. Look, you're here to learn how to be an AD, right?"

"Right, I'm supposed to observe the functions of . . ."

"Then why don't you just sit right down here, and *be* an AD! It's a simple show, and there's nothing like actual experience."

My electronic headache started to throb. My Fruit-of-the-Loom boxer shorts became three sizes too small. I could feel a rash breaking out between my toes. My entire life flashed before my eyes, and I said, "You're talking crazy, sir, whoever you are."

"I'm Vern Diamond. I'm the director of this crappy little show. C'mon, sit down, there's nothing to it."

I think I started to black out. I remember hearing my voice say, "But this is only my second day, Mr. Diamond. . . ."

"Vern, call me Vern. C'mon sit down, I'll tell you what to do."

I sat.

"Now, you see that button in front of you? The one marked Telecini. Just press that, and ask Telecini to light up our opening Telop."

"Button . . . Telecini . . . Telop . . . Light up . . . Right." I couldn't believe these crazy words I was saying. It suddenly occured to me that Vern the director was having a little fun with me. I hoped to God he was.

"Go ahead, Ken, get Telecini. Get with it! We've only got thirty seconds before air!"

He *wasn't* joking. He was deadly serious. I pressed the button marked Telecini. A voice boomed out at me from a loudspeaker. "Go ahead, Studio Seven!"

I pressed the button again. "Is this Telecini?"

The voice boomed again. "Aaaah, c'mon, of course it's Telecini! Who is this, anyway?"

Vern started to scream at me. "The Telop! Tell them to light up the Telop!"

I pressed the button again. "Hello, Telecini . . . Would you . . . would you light up the Telop?" The whole thing sounded so ridiculous I could hardly get the words out of my mouth.

I heard some music coming from somewhere, Vern barked a couple of commands that meant absoutely nothing to me, and

I had a feeling that we were on the air.

Vern turned to me, and said, "There's your opening Telop, right there on the line monitor."

"Line monitor?"

"The TV set in front of us, that's a line monitor."

I looked at the line monitor. There was a drawing of some pots and pans on it.

Vern turned to me. "Ask Telecini to lap the Telop."

I couldn't believe my ears. "I beg your pardon!"

"Tell them to lap the Telop, for chrissakes!"

I flashed a knowing smile at Vern. Now I knew it was a joke. "This is a great gag, Vern. You planned the whole thing, right? I mean it's my first day of observing, and you're giving me the business, right?"

"Are you crazy? What gag? Tell them to lap the Telop! We've been sitting on the title Telop for over a minute!"

"*Lap* the Telop? I can't say a thing like that . . . it sounds dirty."

"Good God Almighty!" Vern leaned over me and pressed the Telecini button. "Lap the Telop, damn it!"

Vern went to work directing his cameras, but I was too flustered to do any observing. During a lull in the proceedings, he said to me, "Lap the Telop means that we want Telecini to dissolve from one Telop to another. I don't know where the term came from, but that's the way it's done."

"Oh."

For the next twenty-six minutes, nothing was required of me, so I just sat there in a semi-daze. I remember promising God that I would start going to Mass again if he'd just get me out of that control room in one piece. I said a few Hail Marys for the quick revival of tap dancing, and I prayed that Vern would not ask me to lap any more Telops. My eyes were hypnotized by the studio clock. All I wanted in life was for that half hour to be over. When the big hand reached five, I started to breathe again, figuring that everything was going to be fine.

"OK, Ken, I've got to put you to work. Call Telecini and ask them to light up our closing Telop."

I pulled myself together, and decided to act like a professional AD. What the hell, I knew all about Telop lapping. Nothing to it!

I pressed the Telecini button. "Hello, Telecini? . . . This is Studio Seven."

"Go ahead, Studio Seven. What can I do for you?"

"Oh, hi there! Could you get me Telecini, I want him to light up our closing Telop."

The voice roared out of the loudspeaker. "What did you say? Is this a gag or something?"

"No, no, I want you to get me Telecini. He's an Italian fellow. I talked to him before."

Suddenly, I sensed that something was wrong. Vern was prostrate over the console, doubled up with laughter. The audio man fell off his chair, and was kneeling on the floor laughing himself into tears. The man I later found out was the technical director raised his arms to the heavens, and screamed, "I've heard everything! . . . I can die happy! . . . I've heard it all." Then *he* burst out laughing.

Three minutes later, when the show got off the air, I still didn't know what they were laughing at. The guys in the control room apologized for laughing at me, then Vern explained that Telecini was the name for the projection room. When they found out that I had never been in a control room before, they were very sympathetic and someone gave me a container of coffee as a gesture of good will.

That was my first experience in television. After all these years, it sounds like a comedy sketch, but while it was happening I had my first bout with "control room stomach," which is a temporary ulcer that stays with you for two hours after you get off the air, or until you get to the nearest bar. The cooking show incident turned out to be a forewarning of things to come.

Incidentally, Vern Diamond, the director, turned out to be a nice guy. I worked with him a few months later, and he wasn't frightening at all. Believe it or not, I think Vern is still directing at CBS.

The Mechanics of the Game

To me, a television control room is something out of an old Buster Crabbe science fiction movie. The racks of tubes, wires, transistors, buttons, knobs, switches, and other mysterious equipment have always intimidated me. I felt this way the first time I entered a control room, and I felt the same way when I walked out of a control room for the last time. I'm sure that the electronic wizards who built and maintained all this equipment felt perfectly at home in a control room. But, to a person like me (I put on rubber gloves when I plug in a floor lamp) the electronic part of television has always been rather frightening.

Except for the director, associate director, and producer,

the control room was the domain of the technician. The technicians all belonged to the same union. The director and associate director belonged to a different union. There was no union for producers, which made them very nervous.

All control rooms had the same ingredients. Some control rooms *looked* different from other control rooms, but they were all the same. There were control rooms with glass partitions, where you could see what went on in the studio. There were control rooms with no glass partition, and you had to guess what was happening in the studio. There were control rooms in the basements of studios, control rooms in the lobbies of converted Broadway theaters, and we had one control room that was located across the street from the studio. But the basic ingredients were there.

The console was the most prominent thing in a control room. "Console" was just a fancy name for a long table with built-in cabinets. Most of the cabinets contained the complicated electronic equipment which controlled the camera switching board. The rest of the console had leg room so that people could sit.

Sitting at the switching board was the technical director. He was the boss of the technical crew, and the one who actually pushed the buttons that put the cameras on the air. Sitting right next to him, usually on his right, was the director. The director told the technical director which button to push. The two of them played the "button game." If the technical director pushed the wrong button, it was scored as one point for the director. If the director made a mistake, and told the technical director to push the wrong button, it was scored as a point for the technical director. If the director told the technical director to push the wrong button, and the technical director pushed the *right* button, it was scored as two points for the technical director. The points were added up after each show, and the final score determined whether the director and technical director would talk to each other for the following week.

On a dramatic show or a situation comedy show, the director had a script in front of him, marked with the camera shots he had rehearsed. A typical page of a director's script for a typical show looked something like page 18:

The notation at the top of the page reminded the director that camera one was on the air, with a two shot of Mark and Riley. Two speeches down the page, he had written a cue to put camera three on the air with a close-up of Barbara. After Barbara's speech, he has a cue to take camera two with a waist shot of Riley. (On a director's script, "T-2"means "take camera two," which means punching up the button that puts camera two on the air.) Two speeches later, the director has written a cue for camera one, which was on the air with a wide three shot, to follow Barbara to the desk. The last two cues on the page are self-explanatory.

The associate director sat on the right side of the director. His job was to tell the cameramen what their next shot was going to be. For instance, if camera two was on the air, and the technical director punched up camera one, camera two became a "released" camera. The associate director would then tell the released cameraman what his next shot was supposed to be. It sounds simple and easy, but it wasn't. To show you what I mean, let's take a look at the same page of dialogue, this time from the associate director's script (see page 19):

At the top of the script page is the usual reminder that they are coming off the preceding page on camera one. Two speeches down the page, the director takes camera three, which releases camera one. The associate director has noted camera one's next shot underneath the "Take 3," and he must get this information to the cameraman as quickly and clearly as he can. In this particular case, he has exactly eleven words of dialogue to give camera one his next shot. At the end of these eleven words, the director takes camera two, camera three becomes the released camera, and the associate director has nine words of dialogue to give camera three his next shot.

This procedure continues down the page, and is repeated on every page of the script. To give you an idea of the quick reflexes needed by an associate director on a dramatic show, try this little game.

Assign three friends to play the roles of Barbara, Mark, and Riley. They don't have to act the parts, all they have to do is read the lines. Then, appoint someone to be the director. He has to read the takes. You play the role of the associate director, and as your friends read their parts, you try to read the notations written underneath the "takes" *before* the director reads *his* next notation.

If you try this, you will find that it is not easy. It requires extreme concentration, fast reflexes, and the ability to talk fast. Stop to consider that this is only one page in a thirty-page script, and you can easily understand why most associate directors were chain smokers.

The wall in front of the console was covered with monitors. It would take ten pages to explain all of them, so I'll just tell you about a few of the most important ones. Right in front of the director and technical director were two monitors that were larger than the others. One was labeled "LINE," and the other "AIR." The line monitor carried the output of the studio. The picture on this monitor was the picture we were sending to the transmitter. The air monitor was a simple television set like the one you have at home. It was there to reassure the workers in the control room that we were on the air and that the viewers were receiving our picture.

Underneath the line monitor were three smaller monitors, marked "Cam 1," "Cam 2," "Cam 3." These were the camera monitors, and they showed the output of each camera. If the technical director wanted to put camera one on the air, he punched camera one's button on the switchboard. The picture on camera one's monitor would then appear on the line monitor, and be sent out to the transmitter.

For the director and associate director, the camera monitors were the most important things in the control room. Every time the associate director gave a released camera his next shot, he had to keep his eye on that camera's monitor, to make sure the cameraman heard him correctly. The director used the camera monitors to play a game with the cameramen. The name of the game was, "Atta boy, aw shit," and it worked like this.

If the director told a cameraman to pan right, ending up with a waist shot of the leading lady, and the cameraman made the move correctly, then the director would say, "Atta boy, Joe, nice move." If the cameraman panned *left,* ending up with a shot of a stagehand picking his nose, the director would then say, "Aw, shit, Joe, that's not the leading lady, that's a stagehand picking his nose!" If a cameraman hit an actor with his camera while making a fast move, that was an "Aw, shit" situation. If the camera did *not* hit an actor with his camera, then he got an "Atta boy, Joe, nice going."

The director would keep score, just as he did with the technical director. The scoring system was simple. Two "Atta boy's" canceled out one "Aw, shit," and everyone started from scratch. If, at the end of a show, a cameraman had three or more "Aw, shit's" next to his name, then the director knew he had an enemy in the studio.

Sitting in a little pit in front of the console were the video men. It was their job to maintain an acceptable picture on the camera monitors, and they did this by constantly turning knobs and watching a dancing green line on an oscilloscope

"SUSPENSE"   SHOW 29   Page 7

(ON #1 - 2 shot M+R)

MARK: Look, officer, I know too many people in this town to
           be threatened by a punk patrolman.

RILEY: I'm not threatening anybody, Mr. Duncan. I'm just
           asking you to come down to the station, and we'll
           straighten out a few things. T-3- cu Barb

BARBARA: He's arresting you, Mark! Are you going to stand for
           that?   T-2 WS Riley

RILEY: Nobody's arresting anybody. I'm just asking you to
           cooperate. T-1 - Wide 3 shot

MARK: Stay out of this, Barbara. I'll handle it.

BARBARA: You're not man enough to handle it! . . . So, I'll
           handle it!   Follow Burb

                    (Barbara runs to desk, opens drawer, and
                     takes out Mark's revolver.)

MARK: Barbara! . . . Are you crazy? T-2 - WS Riley

RILEY: You're acting real silly, Mrs. Duncan. You better
           put that thing away before you get your husband in
           more trouble. T-3 WS Barb

BARBARA: (Pointing gun at Riley) Get out of this house, you
           punk cop! . . . You don't have a warrant, so Mark
           stays right where he is. Now, get out!

"SUSPENSE"   SHOW 29   Page 7

(ON #1 - 2 Shot M + R)

MARK: Look, officer, I know too many people in this town to
            be threatened by a punk patrolman.

RILEY: I'm not threatening anybody, Mr. Duncan. I'm just
            asking you to come down to the station, and we'll
            straighten out a few things.   *T-3 cu Barb*
                                              #1 wide 3 Shot

BARBARA: He's arresting you, Mark! Are you going to stand for
            that?   *T-2 ws Riley*
                      #3 - WS Barbara

RILEY: Nobody's arresting anybody. I'm just asking you to
            cooperate.   *T-1 Wide Shot*
                           #2 - WS Riley

MARK: Stay out of this, Barbara. I'll handle it.

BARBARA: You're not man enough to handle it! . . . So, I'll
            handle it!   *Follow Barb*

                 (Barbara runs to desk, opens drawer, and
                 takes out Mark's revolver.)

MARK: Barbara! . . . Are you crazy?   *T-2 WS Riley*
                                              #1 - TITE gun

RILEY: You're acting real silly, Mrs. Duncan. You better
            put that thing away before you get your husband in
            more trouble.   *T-3 WS Barb*
                              #2 hold

BARBARA: (Pointing gun at Riley) Get out of this house, you
            punk cop! . . . You don't have a warrant, so Mark
            stays right where he is. Now, get out!

type instrument. When they weren't busy doing these things, they cursed the lighting director.

The lighting director usually sat in the rear of the control room for self-protection. Lighting directors and video men were traditionally locked in mortal combat. The video men blamed all of the bad pictures on the lighting director, and credited the good pictures to their own electronic wizardry. The lighting directors claimed that all video men needed a seeing-eye dog to find their way home.

The other member of the control room technical staff was the audio man. He controlled everything you heard on a television show. On a news show, with all the news film sound tracks, he was the busiest man in the control room. On a dramatic show, he was responsible for the mike booms being in the right place at the right times, so that all of the actors' lines were heard clearly and distinctly. If he was doing a musical show, he might have to use fifteen or more mikes to balance out a forty-piece orchestra, and ride herd on twenty additional mikes to put the variety show on the air.

In those days the good audio men had fifteen or twenty years of radio experience behind them, and some of them approached genius. A director never told an audio man *how* to do something. He would tell him what the situation was, and what he expected as a result, but never *how*. The crackerjack audio men spoke only to God. They sat behind their audio boards and were a kingdom unto themselves.

The outsider in the control room was the producer. When the chips were down, if the producer became too critical of the technical crew's work, the director lined up with the technicians and protected them. If a producer tried to crucify a good director, the technical director took the side of the director. There was a good reason for this. It was called "self-preservation." The good directors and associate directors worked very closely with their technical crews. When a director found a crew that he could work with, he protected them with his life. It made the difference between a happy life and ulcers. A good relationship between director and technical crew could save a director's marriage, rescue him from Alcoholics Anonymous, and cut down his intake of sleeping pills. From the crew's point of view, a good director was worth his weight in gold. When a producer had to deal with a director and crew who respected each other, he was often forced to play the role of "that pain in the ass standing in the back of the control room."

I have made no attempt to describe in depth the complicated duties of the men who worked in television control rooms. I simply wanted you to know who they were, what they did, and how they related to each other. At the end of my three week observing period, I knew less than you know now. However, my ignorance did not prevent me from being sent forth into the front lines.

CHAPTER 4

"Strike It Rich"
What it was like to work on the sickest show of the Golden Age

I'd like to say a few words about a TV show that was heartily applauded by network executives, FCC members, city officials, cameramen, and stagehands. The hearty applause was heard on the day that the show was taken off the air.

In the history of show business there have been many violations of good taste. Carnivals and circus shows had their Geeks. The burlesque show had its vulgar blackout sketches. The old minstrel shows featured white men who blackened their faces with burnt cork, and acted out the lie that all blacks were lazy comedians. Broadway has given us "Oh! Calcutta!" But television was responsible for "Strike It Rich."

23

My exposure to "Strike It Rich" was short and merciful. I was assigned to the show as associate director for about two months. A man by the name of Matt Harlib was the director at the time I worked the show. When I say "a man" by the name of Matt Harlib, the choice of words is not accidental. I don't know what became of Matt these last twenty years. I doubt if he is still mixed up in TV. I don't know if he was a talented man, because talent was not required to be the director of "Strike It Rich." I don't know any of these things about Matt Harlib, but there's one thing I do know. He was a man of integrity. He was the only television director I ever heard of who walked out of the control room in the middle of a live show and never came back.

For those of you who are old enough to remember the program, but find that the image is a little fuzzy, let me help jog your memory. "Strike It Rich" was a daily television show that claimed to help the more unfortunate people on earth to a better life. Warren Hull would prance on stage and tell you that "Strike It Rich" existed only to bring a little ray of sunshine into the lives of a few tragedy-struck people. He would then proceed to the interview area, where he would interview some poor son of a bitch who should never have allowed himself to be exploited on a network television show by Warren Hull.

A typical show would start off with a recent double amputee who needed artificial limbs but couldn't afford them. The second guest might have been a black child from Harlem who had seen his mother and father die in a tenement fire. The third receiver of the show's benevolence could have been a destitute farmer from North Carolina who had lost his home and barn in a hurricane. If he was a "good" "Strike It Rich" farmer, the hurricane had also blown away his wife, four cows, and two sons. It's starting to come back to you, right?

After Warren Hull interviewed these poor unfortunates,

bringing out every sordid detail of their tragedy, he would then invite them over to the "Heart Line Area." (Everything on "Strike It Rich" was an "area." If you went to the bathroom during rehearsals, you referred to it as "The Crap House Area.")

The Heart Line Area was a flat piece of scenery with a heart painted on it. The inside of the heart was cut out, and a telephone rested on a small shelf. The Heart Line was the telephone, of course. Various voices would call, offering help to the poor creatures Warren Hull had befriended.

Now you remember it, right?

Some of the Heart Line calls were legitimate. A benevolent surgeon might call up, and offer a free operation to a woman with a bad gall bladder. Or perhaps a kindhearted soul would call and volunteer the bus fare back to Alabama for a sharecropper who had come to New York looking for work.

Some of the Heart Line calls were *not* motivated by an urge to help another human being. They came under the heading of a free plug on network television for a commercial product.

. . . "Hello! . . . Warren Hull? Is this the Heart Line? . . . Well, I'm Richard B. Wilson, president of the Sure Glide Wheel Chair Company . . . I would personally like to help little Johnny recover from his terrible accident . . . So, if little Johnny will come down to our show room at 916 44th Avenue, Jamaica, Queens, New York . . . that's 916 44th Avenue, Jamaica, Queens, New York . . . he will become the proud possessor of a Super Delux Sure Glide Wheel Chair . . . The Super Delux is our luxury model, and I'm sure little Johnny will enjoy all of its advanced features . . . Good luck, Johnny!"

Besides the Heart Line calls from the general public, there were also the "Inside" calls. These calls were usually the voice of a member of the show's staff. These "Inside" calls were made when the outside calls were not coming in fast enough to keep the show going. I saw nothing wrong with the producers making these calls, because I've always believed in the "show must go on" theory. The terrible thing about the "Inside" calls was the stupidity of some of these Heart Line gifts, and the fact that they had the same commercial odor about them.

> "Hello . . . Warren? . . . At this time the producers of 'Strike It Rich' would like to extend a Heart Line to Mrs. Beecher . . . We are giving her a complete set of World Scope Encyclopedias, consisting of thirty volumes . . . World Scope is the most up-to-date encyclopedia set now in print. Its fact-filled pages are generously illustrated with color plates for your education and enjoyment . . . Happy reading, Mrs. Beecher!'
> On too many occasions, Mrs. Beecher was blind.

During the time I worked on "Strike It Rich," the most horrible part of the show was the "morning shape-up" for people who aspired to be on the receiving end of the Heart Line. The official way to get on the show was to send a letter telling your story to the "Strike It Rich" office. If your troubles were sufficiently dramatic, you were invited to come to New York and appear on the show, at your own expense of course. Unfortunately, a great many people thought that if they showed up in person, they would have a better chance of being picked. The result was that twenty or thirty of these unfortunate people would show up at the theater every morning, hoping that they might be the lucky ones.

Although the producers did not encourage this procedure, the hopeful group was always invited back stage, where a member of the production staff would conduct a brief interview session. I never figured out whether the producers were genuinely sympathetic or whether they were afraid they might miss a great participant. Whatever the reason, the results were horrible.

If you have ever been subjected to a mass job interview with twenty other hopefuls, you'll have a slight idea of what it was like. In show business and the modeling profession, this type of thing is called a "cattle call." Among union men on the waterfront, it's called a "shape-up." The cattle call and the shape-up can be the most undignified moment in a person's life, but the interviews conducted every morning on "Strike It Rich" made these experiences seem like eleven o'clock Mass. The applicants involved in the "Strike It Rich" group interviews were not in competition with each other for a job, which is a fairly clean-cut process. Each one of them was matching his own personal tragedy against twenty other personal tragedies for the privilege of appearing on this show. It was grotesque.

Various members of the production staff would conduct these interviews. They rotated, because after one shape-up session, the interviewer would be overcome by a severe case of depression, requiring a twenty-four-hour drink to get it out of his system. A typical session went something like this:

> "Would you all fill out the forms that I've just given you . . . On the top line write your name and address . . . I'll wait . . . How are we doing? . . . Yes, what seems to be the trouble? . . . I understand. Well, don't you worry, I'll fill out the form for you . . . and may I say that 'Strike It Rich' is very partial to

severe arthritis cases. You have an excellent chance of appearing on our show . . . Sir, you seem to be having a problem. Is there any way I can help? . . . You don't KNOW your name and address? . . . An amnesia victim? How dreadful . . . Well, don't you worry about it. Just leave the first line blank. In fact, leave the whole form blank. We'll have to work it out later . . . All right, everybody, fill out the rest of the form, age, occupation, marital status . . . I'll wait . . . Now, let's fill out the last question, 'Why do you want to appear on "Strike It Rich"?' If I can be of any help, please do not hesitate to ask . . . Yes, sir . . . Well, why don't you explain your case to me, and I'll fill it in myself . . . I see, you're a Negro albino . . . Nothing wrong with that, right? Just a quirk of nature, that's all . . . You say that the black community will not tolerate you because you're white . . . Well, that's understandable . . . Oh, I see . . . The white community will not tolerate you because you're TOO white. You certainly have a problem, sir, but I'm afraid it's not a 'Strike It Rich' type of problem . . . No, I have no negative feelings about albinos, some of my best friends are . . .''

And so it went on, every morning.

There was one production assistant who was assigned to run the shape-up twice a month. As far as I know, she never completed an interview session. She would talk to three of the aspirants, and tears would begin sliding down her face. Open weeping would break out a few minutes later, and she would end up sobbing hysterically by the time she had interviewed her fifth victim.

Two days before I was relieved of my duties on "Strike It

Rich," Matt Harlib, the director, made his beautiful move. We were doing one of our typical shows. Matt was taking the usual camera shots. Close-ups of weeping people as they exposed their tragedies to Warren Hull, and wide shots of the audience as they applauded the weeping people . . . Just an ordinary show.

The third and last victim on this particular show was a sixty-five-year-old paraplegic who was paralyzed from the waist down. Warren conducted his usual warm interview:

> ". . . So, up until the tragic accident nine months ago, you were a healthy vigorous lumberjack . . . Now, you are a helpless shell of a man, unable to support your family . . . Well, believe me, sir, you have come to the right place . . . STRIKE IT RICH IS HERE TO HELP YOU! . . . [Wild applause from the audience] . . . Now, Mr. Cullen, if you will step over to the Heart Line Area, we'll make sure that you STRIKE IT RICH!"

Warren Hull then walked briskly to the Heart Line Area, obviously forgetting that Mr. Cullen was a paraplegic. Mr. Cullen stared across the stage at Mr. Hull for a few embarrassing moments. Mr. Hull stared across the stage at Mr. Cullen for a few embarrassing moments. Then, Mr. Cullen realized that something was expected of him. He planted his crutches firmly in front of him, pulled himself out of the chair, and started his slow, painful journey across the stage to the Heart Line Area.

At that moment, I realized that I was witness to the high point of low taste in the entertainment industry. It suddenly occurred to me that I was working on a Geek show. The cameraman on camera two grabbed a tight shot of Mr. Cullen's legs

"Now, Mr. Cullen, if you will step over to the Heart Line Area, we'll make sure that you STRIKE IT RICH!"

as they scraped their way across the stage. One of the bosses standing in the back of the control room yelled, "Take two, Matt! Take two!"

Matt looked at the shot on camera two, and turned to the voice from the back of the control room. On his face was a look of utter disbelief. "You really want me to put that shot on the air?"

"It's a great shot, Matt! A tight shot of the crutches *and* the legs! It's fantastic!"

Matt took one more look at the shot on camera two, then he got up from the director's chair, took off his head set, and walked out of the control room.

He never came back.

CHAPTER 5

"The Garry Moore (Daytime Version) Show"

The Garry Moore daytime show was my first permanent assignment at CBS. It turned out to be the most fortunate assignment of my television career.

Before going to work for Garry, my associate directing jobs had been a hit-or-miss proposition. I had a different schedule every day, and I never knew *what* I would be doing the following week. During those early months, a typical schedule would have me doing "Strike It Rich" in the morning, a cooking show hour later, a daytime quiz show in the afternoon, and possibly a news show in the evening. Sometimes I was assigned to shows that I had never even *seen*. When this happened, I lost

33

a lot of sleep, and asked a lot of questions.

I don't know who was responsible for my assignment to "The Garry Moore Show." I know it wasn't an accident, because later on I found out that the show had put in a request for an associate director who could stage and choreograph song numbers. (Some of you middle-aged fossils might remember that the two singers on the show were Denise Lor and Ken Carson.)

Now, this chapter may bore you to death, because I'm going to talk about a group of good people. There wasn't one person connected with "The Garry Moore Show" who was evil, or neurotic, or just plain unfriendly. Everyone on the show was a professional, and very secure in their abilities and their jobs.

The producer was Herb Sanford, an old friend of Garry's from the early radio days in Chicago. Herb was a sweet old guy who used to sit in the back of the control room and doze off while we were on the air. During production meetings, he was very much the producer. At these planning sessions he would sit at the head of the table, and run things with a soft iron hand. But, once the show went on the air, he seemed to lose interest. He would watch the first ten minutes with mild concern, then he would drop off to sleep.

I didn't know it at the time, but that's *exactly* what a good producer should do. Old Mr. Sanford was a wise man. He knew that he should prepare the best show he could. He also knew that once a show went on the air, he was helpless.

It was a truth that very few television producers seemed to be aware of. Most of the producers I encountered did exactly the opposite. During the preparation period and the planning sessions, this type of producer would voice very few opinions and very few ideas. He would sit in the background during these creative meetings, order coffee for everyone, agree with everyone, then buy drinks for everyone at an East Side cocktail lounge.

Once we were on the air with the show, this type of producer would suddenly come to life with opinions, ideas, helpful hints, and criticism . . . especially criticism. These guys were not producers at all. They were critics. When the sheet of paper was blank, they had no idea how to fill it. But, once the paper had something written on it, they were always ready to correct the spelling. Herb Sanford was not one of these gents. I wish more producers had dozed off while their shows were on the air. . . . It might have saved me the embarrassment of using hair dye before the age of thirty.

Clarence Schimmel was the director, and if my memory serves me right, I think he directed all of Garry's daytime shows for the many years he was on the air. Clarence didn't have a show business background, but he was a good control room director, and the perfect man for this kind of show. Right now, in 1972, he's teaching a television production course at Brooklyn College. I haven't seen Clarence for more than fifteen years, but I know his students are getting the right information, because I know how much he taught *me*.

On the other side of the cameras was Durward Kirby, the second most important member of the Garry Moore "family." Durward was the comic element in the show, and acted out the role of Garry's goofball announcer and friend. If you are as old as I am, and if you watched daytime television in 1951, you might remember that Garry Moore never claimed to be a comedian. He never told jokes, he never dressed up in women's clothes to do a sketch, and he left the punch lines to Durward. Garry was a "reactor." In show business, a "reactor" is usually the "second banana." On "The Garry Moore Show," the "reactor" was the "first banana." Sounds complicated, but you've seen this set-up many times, whether you are aware of it or not. For instance, Jackie Gleason was a first banana who "reacted" to Art Carney, who was a "second banana." Gleason would feed

Carney a straight line or a question. Carney would give out with his answer and get a laugh, then Gleason would react with one of his great facial expressions that indicated disgust, or disbelief, or frustration, or any other emotion that Gleason wished to communicate. The reaction would get just as big a laugh as Carney's funny line, and the process would start all over again.

Laurel and Hardy were great exponents of this method of comedy, and you can see a good example of it any night you turn on Johnny Carson's show. Carson is one of the best men in the business with a funny line, or a monologue. He also happens to be the best ad-libber in the business. But, if you watch carefully, you'll notice that forty percent of Carson's comedy is based on reactions to guests and to Ed McMahon.

Anyway, that's the way Garry and Durward worked. Durward was the big woolly bear who made wisecracks and gave out with the dumb answers. Garry would respond with a funny, but kind reaction, like an understanding father watching his son make a fool of himself. Ken Carson, the male singer on the show, played the other son. Denise Lor was the daughter.

On the air the show projected a family feeling. It looked as if Garry, the father, had gathered the family together for a few laughs, and to meet some interesting guests. The show was warm, relaxed, amusing, educational, and it was professional all the way.

For the first couple of months I couldn't figure out what Garry Moore was *selling*. Oh, I don't mean the products in the commercials. I'm talking about what part of *himself* he was selling. Every performer who gets up on a stage, stands in front of a movie camera, or enters your living room on television is selling himself in some way.

If he claims to be a juggler, then he'd better juggle pretty well. If he is not a clever juggler, then he has to be very funny when he makes a mistake. If a movie starlet claims to be an actress, and she is not a good actress, then she better have big mammary glands. I mean, you've got to have *something* to sell.

For a while, I didn't know *what* Garry Moore was selling. As I said, he certainly made no attempt to be a comedian. When he was funny, it looked like an accident. When he interviewed a guest, it didn't sound like an interview. It sounded more like a conversation in a bar, or a couple of people chewing the fat on a back porch. He wasn't a singer, *that's* for sure. And his dancing ability was confined to one single tap dancing step which threatened a trip to the hospital every time he made an attempt.

Slowly but surely I became aware of what Garry really *did* on the show. When he was funny and it looked as it wasn't planned, it *was* planned. When the interviews sounded like he was shooting the bull with the guy next door, it was because he *wanted* it to sound that way. When he horsed around with Durward, you believed that the two of them were pals since childhood. It wasn't true.

The truth was that Garry was a very talented performer. He just didn't advertise the fact. He underplayed all of his talents, which was exactly right for a show that went on the air at ten o'clock in the morning.

There's one more talent that Garry had, and it might have been his biggest talent. Well, maybe "talent" isn't the right word. It was more of a quality in his personality. But, whatever it was, I think it was the main thing that Garry was selling. Garry sold love. Crazy, uh? But it was true. He could project warmth and affection into a television camera, through the telephone cables, and spill it into living rooms all over the country. He made millions of people feel better about the day they were facing. . . . And that wasn't a bad talent to have.

As I said before, the whole feeling of the show was that of a family having a good time. If you watched the show every day

"He sold love." (Honest to God!)

for a week, you would have believed that the four of them ate breakfast, lunch, and dinner together. They related to each other so well in front of the cameras that most viewers believed they were just as intimate in real life, which wasn't true.

They were friendly, of course. They liked each other, and they respected each other's talents, but, once they left the studio, they certainly didn't hang around with each other. Each of them led their own lives for twenty-one hours of the day. Then, for the two hours leading up to the air show, they treated each other as professionals. For one hour a day, while they were on the air, they became the family. It worked fine.

Ken Carson was the one person in the family that didn't seem to fit with the other three members. He was a prairie type guy who looked like a cowboy when he was wearing a tuxedo. He sang pop songs with a western twang, and accompanied himself on the guitar. During the time I worked with him, I knew very little about him. Come to think of it, I don't even know if he was married or not. He showed up at the studio every day carrying his guitar, and looking like a rodeo star on a day off. After the show was over, he'd pack up his guitar and disappear.

Ten years after "The Garry Moore Show," had gone off the air, I finally got to know a little bit about Ken Carson. I bumped into him at an East Side bar one night. We were both miserable, and we both wanted to drink. In an hour and a half, we consumed nine martinis served in glasses that were big enough to raise tropical fish.

During the hour and a half we decided that television was a pain in the ass, agents were a double pain in the ass, women were a triple pain in the ass, and show business in general shouldn't even be discussed.

"The whole thing's crazy," said Carson, as he missed his mouth with a handful of peanuts.

"Agreed," I said. "You name it, and it's a pain in the ass."

"I've got to be nuts. . . . I mean, what I'm trying to do. . . . I gotta be nuts."

I removed the three olives from my martini, and pondered his statement. This particular bar always put three olives in the martinis, and I was afraid that the olives would soak up too much alcohol. I didn't want to miss the purpose of the martini.

"Naw, you're not nuts," I said. "Show business is nuts. Do you know that I could meet you here in this bar one year from now, and you could be a big star."

"That's what's nuts. I don't want to be a big star."

I removed two of Carson's peanuts from my pants cuff. "I agree with you, that's really crazy. What the hell are you doing in show business if you don't want to be a big star?"

"Well, you won't believe this," he said. "You're *really* going to think I'm crazy."

Carson turned to me with a serious expression on his face. He looked like a nine-year-old kid who was going to confession for the first time and was about to admit that he played with himself.

"You know what I'm doing in show business? You really want to know why I'm knocking my brains out in this stupid business? I'm trying to put together enough money to buy a ranch. . . . That's crazy, isn't it?"

"What's crazy about that?" I said. "Lots of show business people buy ranches . . . or farms . . . places like that. . . . What's crazy about it?"

"But I *had* a ranch! . . . When I was a kid my father owned a ranch. . . . I left the ranch to go into show business. . . . And now I'm in show business so I can buy a ranch. . . . That's crazy, right?"

"Right, that's crazy."

We both had another fish bowl full of martini. Carson sat there staring at the bottles in back of the bar, but his eyes weren't focused on the bottles. He was looking at a ranch somewhere in Wyoming or Arizona.

I couldn't even see the bottles.

I finished my martini, and started to eat the olives that were spread out on the napkin in front of me. I figured that they must have soaked up *some* of the alcohol.

After four olives, I said, "You know why I'm knocking my brains out trying to direct television shows?"

"Beats the hell out of *me*," said Carson. "That's a *real* ridiculous profession."

"I'm trying to save enough money to buy a gray-shingled house by the edge of the sea in Marshfield, Massachusetts . . . . I think I want to be a lobsterman."

"Nothing wrong with that. . . . Lots of money in lobsters."

"I was brought up in Marshfield, Massachusetts."

"Oh."

"Crazy, uh?"

"Something like that."

That was the last time I ever saw Ken Carson. I hope he got his ranch. Incidentally, I don't think I mentioned it before, but Ken was a very talented singer. And incidentally, I still don't have a gray-shingled house by the edge of the sea in Marshfield, Massachusetts.

Whenever I think of the Garry Moore daytime show, one particular incident always comes to my mind. It happened while Clarence Schimmel, the regular director, was on vacation. Garry let me direct the show while Clarence was gone. One day, I planned a rather ambitious setting for one of Denise Lor's song numbers. I wanted Denise to be sitting on the edge of a swimming pool while she sang her number. I wanted to see the water in the pool, I wanted to see the tiled edge of the pool, and I wanted to see Denise dangling her feet in the water.

With the budget we were allowed on the show, these wants were pretty damn impossible. Luckily, the scenic designer and set dresser were dedicated gentlemen, so the three of us together worked out a cheap way to get the effect I wanted. The scenic designer came up with a water pan that measured six feet by eight feet, was twelve inches deep, and rented for twenty dollars. The set dresser worked his magic, dreaming up a mixture of platforms, phony tiles that were glued on the platforms, and some outdoor furniture to back up the whole scene. It was a triumph of talent over budget.

On the day of this particular show, everything arrived on time. We had a whole hour to set up our swimming pool scene. The stagehands were enthusiastic as they placed the water pan, set up the platforms, and glued the phony tiles. It was fun. We all felt as if we were creating something.

When the whole thing was finished, we all stood back and admired our creation. It looked perfect. To check it out, I ran into the control room and looked at the camera shot that I had planned. It *was* perfect. It looked exactly the way I wanted it to. With one exception . . . there was no water in the water pan.

That's when the trouble started. I bounced out of the control room happy as a lark. I leaped up on stage feeling like John Huston. "Looks like a million bucks," I yelled. "Great! Only thing missing is the water. . . . OK, fellas, fill up the water pan."

The enthusiasm drained out of the stagehands with a sudden rush. Not one of them made a move to fill up the water pan. They just stood there, giving each other dirty looks, and mumbling things under their breath. They also gave *me* a few dirty looks.

After a minute or so of this, I screamed in my best directorial tone of voice, "What's the matter? What's the problem? Are we gonna fill up the water pan, or are we *not* going to fill up the water pan! What's the big deal?"

"It's a jurisdictional problem, Ken," said one of the stagehands. "Nothing personal . . . it's not your problem."

"What do you mean it's not my problem? I don't want to go on the air with a *dry* swimming pool! I've got two shots of Denise swishing her feet around in the water. If we don't have any water, what the hell is she going to swish her feet around *in?*"

"It's a jurisdiction thing, Ken," said one of the old-timers. "We have the electric department, the prop department, and the carpentry department. . . . Each department has its own responsibility."

"Big news! . . . Who the hell do you think you're talking to? . . . Remember *me?* . . . I used to be in show business! I went to your son's wedding in 1939, right? . . . And you're standing there trying to explain the stagehand union! I know all about the stagehand union, and if you don't fill up that water pan, I sure as hell won't show up at your *grandson's* wedding!"

"You're getting pissed off," said the old-timer. "No sense in that. . . . It's our problem."

"But what's the problem? . . . I don't get it."

"Nobody wants to fill up the water pan, Ken. . . . The prop department won't touch it. . . . The carpenters don't want any part of it . . . and the electrical guys said no."

"This is ridiculous! We've done water pans before! You've filled them up!"

"They were *little* water pans, Ken. . . . We did it as a favor."

"What's so big about this little water pan, may I ask?"

"You're starting to talk Jewish, Ken, and it's not going to help. . . . This is a *big* water pan. Six feet by eight feet, and twelve inches deep. . . . That's a lot of water."

"What's the big deal?" I begged. "We've got a hose all ready for you. All you've got to do is turn it on, and fill up the water pan!"

"That's not what they object to, Ken. . . . We'll fill it up in ten minutes. No problem at all, but who's going to *empty* it?"

"Aw, c'mon, guys. . . . Fill up the water pan, uh? . . . As a personal favor . . . . Look, don't think of me as a director, do it for an ex-tap dancer . . . . OK?"

"There you go getting personal again. It's strictly jurisdictional. The guys that fill the pan have to empty it, and nobody will touch it."

I stopped groveling and went back to being a director. "Call Yaeger! . . . Get Yaeger on the phone, and get him down here!" (Yaeger was the boss of Local One of the stagehand union.)

"Cut it out, Ken. . . . Yaeger's not going to come over here."

"You call him, or I call him! I'm going to get that water pan filled."

The head carpenter reluctantly headed for the phone. "Swimming pool, you mean. That thing is either a *little* swimming pool, or a *big* water pan."

Fifteen minutes later, Mr. Yaeger arrived on the scene. I explained the situation to him, and then the stagehands explained the situation to him. He stared at both factions for a couple of seconds, walked over to a fire bucket filled with sand, spat in the bucket, and then returned to center stage.

"You have a problem here. . . . No doubt about that. A legitimate problem." He turned to me. "Ken, these men are right. . . . They're not trying to shaft you, they're just good union men with a problem. There is no jurisdictional ruling in our union about filling water pans."

"But, who *not*, for God's sake! Water pans are part of television!"

"Well, it's a baby industry, Ken. . . . We just haven't filled that many water pans. . . . The problem has never come up."

"Well, it's come up *now*, Mr. Yaeger! I've got a *dry* water pan sitting over there, Mr. Yaeger! What are you going to do about it?"

Yaeger stared at me for a long, cold six seconds. "I'm going to make a ruling, *Mr.* Whelan."

He turned to face the stagehands. "Men, two of your departments are going to be happy about my ruling, and one department might not vote for me in the next union elections . . . but, I think it's a ruling that's based on pure logic. . . . Here it is. . . . From now on, the filling of water pans is under the jurisdiction of the electrical department."

The three members of the electrical department responded with the following comments:

"Aw, for crisesakes!"

"Pure logic, bullshit!"

"You've just lost *my* vote, Yaeger."

The members of the prop and carpentry departments reacted in a different way.

"That's using the old brain, Yaeger."

"Next election, I'll vote for you *twice.*"

"That's what this union needs, a little more Jewish logic."

"Let's hear it for Yaeger! . . . *Our* boss!"

The number one man in the electrical department asked the one question we all wanted to ask. "OK, you've made the decision . . . but, would you please let us in on the *pure logic?*

. . . I mean, what the hell has the electrical department got to do with filling water pans?"

"Very simple," said Yaeger. "What is the primary source of electricity . . . the *very* primary source of electricity?" Yaeger put on his coat, took one more spit in the fire bucket, then relit his cigar. "*Water* is the primary source of electricity! Water power is what makes those dynamos run! It's pure logic!" He shook everybody's hand but mine and started for the stage door. His parting remark was a gem. "Now, we all understand this, right? From now on, the filling of water pans is the electrical department's responsibility. . . . That's the ruling. . . . At least, for *today* that's the ruling."

You have to respect a guy like that.

A whole book could be done about Yaeger and Local One of the stagehand union, especially during the early years of television. He was deadly in negotiation with management, using his quick mind, his stubborn aggressiveness, and his pure logic to win points for "his boys." I had many arguments with Mr. Yaeger, and there were moments when I wished he didn't exist. But, when he died many years ago, I discovered that I missed him. . . . And I wasn't even one of "his boys."

For a director or associate director, one of the most nerve-wracking things about live television was a live commercial. You don't see them anymore; they're extinct. Oh, maybe there's a local station in Iceland that still does live commercials for the neighborhood hardware store, but on network television, the live commercial is gone forever.

The Garry Moore daytime show had *lots* of live commercials. In fact, Garry encouraged them. The show was one hour long, and if my memory is correct, we did five or six live commercials during that hour. I think the reason Garry liked to do live commercials was that they gave Durward and himself more opportunities to relate to each other, and to perform. I'm sure that Garry regarded live commercials as "material."

We did some of the most ambitious live commercials ever done on television. Most of them were done in the form of little sketches involving Garry and Durward. They were charming, funny, and they sold products. Incidentally, Garry Moore was one of the few television personalities I worked with who would not endorse a product he didn't believe in. I know for a fact that he refused many sponsors because he didn't like what they were selling. It was integrity carried to a point just short of hari-kari.

Live commercials were a pain in the neck for many reasons. For instance, when you did a live commercial you could always depend on advertising agency people showing up in droves. On "The Garry Moore Show," one live commercial meant three or four agency "supervisors" in the studio. When you consider that we did five or six commercials a day, you can well imagine the invasion of Madison Avenue folk. Sometimes there were more agency people in the studio than there were people in the audience.

Another reason why live commercials were an ulcer-making proposition was the naive attitude of the agency people who wrote the commercials. Sometimes I wondered if any of them had ever been in a television studio. It seemed to me that the majority of these agency writers were extremely illogical about the whole thing. If I had been making a living writing live commercials for "The Garry Moore Show," I think I would have dropped into the studio at least *once,* just to look at the set-up and see how we operated. Yet this fairly logical action very seldom happened. The hordes of agency people we encountered in the studio were *not* the people who created the commercials, they were the supervisors who were supposed to police the commercial, and see that everything was carried out to the letter.

The results were sometimes disastrous, sometimes funny, but always murder on the director's digestive system.

The one live commercial that I shall never forget happened on the Garry Moore summer replacement show in 1952. It was my first real shot at directing a network television show, and at that stage of the game, I really didn't *need* an incident like this.

It was a live commercial for a carpet manufacturer. I'm not going to mention the name of the company, which I remember very well, because it wasn't their fault. It was the agency's fault, and I *don't* remember *what* agency, because I've suppressed it with the help of a very expensive psychiatrist.

I received the commercial copy at four o'clock in the afternoon, the day before we were supposed to air the thing. I read it quickly, and by the time I got to the middle of the second page, I knew we were in deep trouble. For three very important reasons:

FIRST,

a live television commercial usually ran one minute. Sometimes they ran fifty-eight seconds, for reasons beyond our control. Sometimes they ran one minute and ten seconds, due to no fault of mine. But they *never* ran four minutes. The copy for the carpet commercial was four-and-a-half pages long, and figuring one minute a page, I knew we had a big problem.

SECONDLY,

the commercial copy had *no* camera directions, nor did it give any hint about what was supposed to *happen* during the commercial. It was simply four-and-a-half pages of announcer's copy, explaining the virtues of a rug.

THIRDLY,

attached to this script was a short note with the following information: "The announcer will be in the
studio at 8:30 A.M. in case you wish to talk to him
before rehearsal. The baby and the dog will arrive at
9:00 o'clock."

I spent the next half hour trying to figure out what the hell
they were talking about. First I'd read the copy, then I'd read
the note. When I didn't get any results that way, I tried reading the note first, and then the copy. At the end of the half
hour I gave up. I could find nothing in the copy that had anything to do with a baby or a dog.

Finally, in exasperation, I called the agency to see if they
could give me a little more information. I talked to eleven people and not one of them knew anything about a baby or a dog.
In fact, there was a great deal of skepticism about the agency
having a carpet company for a client.

I was completely bewildered, so on the way home I did
what I always do when I'm completely bewildered. . . . I
stopped at a bar and enlisted the logic of seven martinis. When
I left the bar, I was still baffled, but I didn't care.

At eight-thirty the next morning, the announcer for the
carpet commercial showed up on schedule.

"Hi. . . . You the director?"

"Yes."

"I'm the voice-over guy for the carpet thing. . . . Glad to
meet you."

"And *I'm* glad to meet *you.* . . . What is this bullshit
about a baby and a dog?"

He looked at me with a different kind of look. His eyes
went on guard, as if he suddenly suspected he might be talking
to a mental case, but wasn't sure. "I beg your pardon?"

"The baby and the dog! . . . Where the hell do they fit into this commercial?"

"Beats the hell out of *me*. . . . A baby and a dog? . . . That's what you said, right? . . . A baby and a dog. . . . No, I don't know anything about that."

"It's ridiculous! . . . This whole thing is absolutely crazy!"

"Yes, it's beginning to sound that way." His eyes became a little more guarded than they were before.

"Didn't the agency *talk* to you about the commercial? Didn't they *explain* what it was all about?"

"No, they just handed me this three-act play which explains how they weave a rug. . . . It seems to me that it's a little too long."

"It's a *lot* too long! It's three minutes too long! And, what about the goddamn baby and the dog?"

The announcer retreated out the stage door, mumbling something about breakfast, and that he couldn't work on an empty stomach.

At nine o'clock sharp, a baby, a dog, a mother, and a trainer showed up. The mother went with the baby, the trainer went with the dog. I ignored all four of them until the agency people arrived.

"The carpet people, I presume."

"Right you are," answered one of them. "Are you the director?"

"Yes, I'm Ken Whelan. Glad to meet you. . . . Now, let's step out in the lobby and have a little talk. We have a coffee urn out there with some doughnuts and danish. . . . We'll just talk this thing over in a nice friendly way."

After I settled them down with their coffee and pastry, I started in, slow and cautious. "Gentlemen, never in my television career have I encountered a commercial as ridiculous as *this* one!"

"I beg your pardon!" said one of them with a mouth full of prune danish.

"In the first place, you've bought *one* minute of air time, and your copy runs *four* minutes!"

"That's impossible!" said the leader.

"It's four-and-a-half pages long!"

"But, the typing is double spaced. . . . You must be wrong."

"Oh, dear God! Didn't you *time* it?"

"No. . . . It seemed all right."

At this point, a dark thought started to form in the back of my mind. I put my own container of coffee back on the table, and the terrible thought became verbal. "Gentlemen, a suspicion has just crossed my mind, and I pray that it is a symptom of paranoia. . . . It has just occurred to me that this might be the first television commercial your agency has ever attempted. . . . Tell me I'm wrong. . . . Please!"

They all looked at each other, and the answer was written on their attaché cases.

"You're kidding," I said. *"This* is the *first?"*

"I'm afraid so," said the leader.

I went back to the table for my coffee, hoping that the coffee had magically turned into a container of straight gin. "That's swell. . . . That's really great. A virgin agency, and you pick a very popular network show to get deflowered. . . . Couldn't you have practiced a little on *local* shows?"

They just sat there and stared at me.

"Well, if that's the way it is, we'll just try to do the best we can. . . . First, we've got to cut your four pages down to one-and-a-half pages, and then . . . Wait a minute! No, that can wait. . . . The *first* thing is the baby and the dog! Tell me about the baby and the dog."

The hostile looks disappeared, and they all smiled at me.

It was a proud smile, as if I had asked them to show me pictures of their kids.

"That was Dave's idea," said the leader, obviously very pleased with himself and Dave. "You see, we didn't want the announcer to appear in the camera shot. We wanted something a little different, something a little more creative. So Dave came up with this . . ."

"Tell me about the baby and the dog."

"Well, Dave had this fabulous idea about . . ."

"What do they *do? . . .* What in the hell do they *do?*"

"Oh, it's very simple. That's what so beautiful about Dave's idea, it's so simple. You see, you start on a camera shot of the rug . . ."

"Makes sense."

"Then you tilt the camera over to a shot of the baby . . ."

"Pan."

"What?"

"We pan cameras, we truck cameras, and we dolly cameras . . . but we never *tilt* cameras. . . . OK, I pan over to the baby. What's the baby doing?"

"The baby is sitting on our beautiful rug playing with its toys. . . . Then we cue the dog to come in. This is the best part of Dave's idea. . . . The dog walks over to the baby, licks the baby's face, then sits down on the rug beside the baby."

"What? . . . The dog does *what?*"

"The dog sits down on the rug beside the baby."

"Not that part! The other part! Did you say that the dog walks in and *licks the baby's face?*"

"Yes. Isn't that a wonderful touch? It's so warm."

"You're crazy! . . . *You* are crazy, *Dave* is crazy . . . you're *all* crazy! . . . How the hell are you going to get a dog to do that? This is a live commercial! We get one shot at it . . . . Just one!"

"Don't worry about it. . . . We had a long talk with the

dog trainer, and there's no problem. . . . You see, the trainer smears the baby's face with bacon grease, and the dog automatically licks off the bacon grease."

"Bacon grease? . . . I don't believe this! . . . What if the dog *doesn't* lick the bacon grease? What if he automatically eats the goddamn baby's head off?"

"This is a trained dog, Mr. Whelan."

"Terrific."

The way it turned out, we never did get around to rehearsing the baby and the dog. It took us more than an hour to cut the four pages of copy down to the required length, and by the time we finished, it was time to go on the air. To be truthful, I don't think I *wanted* to rehearse the baby and the dog. I just didn't want to meet a stage mother who would allow her six-month-old baby to be rubbed with bacon grease so she could boast to her neighbors that her child was in show business.

On the air, the commercial was a disaster. The only *good* thing about it was the fact that the dog did not chew up the baby in front of several million viewers. At least *that* was a plus.

I opened up with the shot of the rug, and cued the announcer. After a few lines of copy I panned the camera to the baby. The baby was *not* sitting on the rug playing with its toys. It was sitting on the rug staring right into the camera. The bacon grease was dripping off its little chin, making the baby look like a well-basted turkey ready to be popped into the oven. The well-greased baby stared into the camera for ten or fifteen seconds, then lost its balance and rolled over on its side like a felled deer.

When I cued the dog to come in, he ran across the rug as if he was chasing a cat. He completely ignored the baby, and headed for camera three, which he used for a hydrant. His appearance in the camera shot was exactly one second long.

We still had forty seconds left in the commercial, and I was stuck with a shot of this crazy baby lying on the rug crying its eyes out. It was at this point that Dave, the creative agency fellow who had invented this whole mess, made an excellent suggestion.

"Get the camera off that stupid baby! It looks like the rug is making him cry!"

I did what he asked, and for thirty long seconds the CBS Television Network filled the airways with a camera shot of a rug.

Needless to say, we lost the client, we lost the agency, and I lost a little prestige. In true television fashion, the agency blamed the whole thing on "an untalented and rude director." I would just like to say one thing before I end this story, and it's this:

"Dave, you no good son of a bitch! May you end up working for an ad agency located somewhere within the Arctic Circle!"

"The Garry Moore Show" spoiled me. Everybody on the show was sane, and it led me to believe that it was always going to be like this. There were no phonies, no back clappers, no put downers and second guessers. There were just talented people who treated each other with respect. And it spoiled me.

CHAPTER **6**

"The Jackie Gleason Show"

If you were the associate director of "The Jackie Gleason Show" for two years, you were bound to bump into Jackie Gleason once in a while. But it wouldn't mean that you knew him. So if you're expecting some juicy bits of inside information about Jackie's personal life, you're barking up the wrong associate director.

When I say that I was the associate director of the show for two seasons, you might think I spent long hours with Jackie's production staff, and participated in days of rehearsal prior to the actual show. You would be wrong. I spent exactly one day a week on the show, and that was Saturday, the day it went on the air. When I walked into the studio on Saturday morning, I had no more idea of what was on tap than the Greek guy who delivered the coffee. I wasn't the only one who started from scratch on Saturday morning. The technical crew very seldom knew what was going to happen, and sometimes even the director was in the dark. The most informed people in the studio were the stagehands, because they knew what sets had been delivered to the studio the night before.

The two years I worked on the show were Gleason's first two years at CBS, after his move from Dumont. These were the early years when he was doing his great characters like the Poor Soul, Reggie Van Gleason, and the Honeymooners. Later on, when videotape was invented, he taped half-hour versions of the Honeymooners, and later than that, he taped one-hour musical comedy shows based on the Honeymooners. I may be prejudiced, but I think that those first two years at CBS were Gleason's best years. They were hectic and insane years, but the fact that the shows were live, and that Jackie knew that he was playing not only to the studio audience but to millions of people out there in the dark, seemed to make him rise to the height of his talent. When I say, "I may be prejudiced," don't think for a moment that I enjoyed working on the Gleason show for two years. I didn't. It was awful.

There is no way that I can talk about "The Jackie Gleason Show" during these two years without first telling you about "Frankenstein." Frankenstein was the director. That wasn't his real name, of course, it was his nickname. There's no point mentioning his real name, because it wouldn't mean anything. His television directing career was short—thank God.

Frankenstein was a tall good-looking Jewish guy and a very likable fellow—outside of the television studio.

Frankenstein's approach to television directing was

unique. Most directors of variety formats like the Gleason show wanted every scrap of information they could get about what was going to happen on the show. If there wasn't time to rehearse a sketch or musical number on camera, the director would talk it over with as many people as he could find in an effort to get a general idea of what was going to take place. Frankenstein's method was quite different, and refreshingly simple. He didn't want to know *anything* about the show. He avoided information like the plague. If there was a Honeymooners sketch on the show, he didn't want to look at the script or even have the script in front of him during air time. We finally came to the conclusion that Frankenstein believed in elves. We decided that he was truly a man of faith, and that when he walked into the control room at eight o'clock on Saturday nights, it was with complete trust that the elves would put the show on the air.

After working with him for a month we realized that we were right. Frankenstein *did* believe in elves. Then we realized that *we* were the elves.

Elf number one was Bob Daily, an extremely talented technical director. (Ted Miller was the technical director for the second year . . . equally talented.) Elf number two was me. The rest of Frankenstein's elves were three clever cameramen, a great audio man, and a couple of mike boom men who could think for themselves. Every once in a while we played a game with him. We would all take turns trying to get Frankenstein to accept just one piece of information, or make one decision. The game went something like this:

B. DAILY:

"Frankenstein, if Gleason moves too far outside that door, we won't be able to cover him with a mike."

FRANKENSTEIN:

"Right, Bob . . . Make a note of that, and be sure that the audio man tells Gleason." (This was a strikeout for B. Daily, because Frankenstein was no longer responsible for this problem.)

*   *   *

LIGHTING DIRECTOR:

"Frankenstein, where do you want that light cue in the dance number? Is it after the first sixteen bars, or after the first chorus?"

FRANKENSTEIN:

"Right, Herb . . . How's the wife?"

LIGHTING DIRECTOR:

"Fine, but . . ."

FRANKENSTEIN:

"When are you going to invite me up to the house for the weekend? I could use a couple of days in the country."

LIGHTING DIRECTOR:

"Any time, Frankenstein, any time. Now about the . . ."

FRANKENSTEIN:

"I'll take you up on that, Herb. You're doing a helluva job, Herb, a helluva job. See you later." (This was a double strikeout for Herb Alexander, the lighting director. He not only failed to get a decision from

Frankenstein, he might even get stuck with him for a whole weekend.)

*   *   *

ME:

"Frankenstein, have you got a minute? I think you've got a problem."

FRANKENSTEIN:

"I don't want to know about problems, you know that. . . . I work better when my mind is uncluttered."

ME:

"You've still got a problem."

FRANKENSTEIN:

"That's ridiculous, I'm the director. What kind of a problem?"

ME:

"A timing problem."

FRANKENSTEIN:

"A timing problem? . . . I can't believe my ears! . . . My favorite associate director comes to me, and tells *me* that *I've* got a timing problem! You know very well that timing the show is *your* responsibility. I'm a little shaken by this, Ken."

ME:

"Your car is parked in front of the loading ramp,

they can't get the scenery into the theater, there's a fire hydrant two feet from your car, and there are four cops about to tow your car away. . . . If you *time* it right, you can beat them to it."

FRANKENSTEIN:

"Take care of it, Ken. A good associate director is responsible for *all* timing problems." (He drifted away to talk to a June Taylor dancer.)

*   *   *

Now, it may sound as if Frankenstein was a bad choice to direct "The Jackie Gleason Show." After all, it went on the air at eight o'clock Saturday nights in prime time, it received great ratings, and a lot of money was involved. It would seem that a more talented director could have made the show even more successful than it was. Logic would dictate that a creative director who understood comedy and who assumed the responsibility for his decisions would have been a big asset to the show.

Logic is wrong: Frankenstein was an excellent choice to direct "The Jackie Gleason Show."

In the first place, Mr. Gleason didn't *want* a director. In the second place, Mr. Gleason didn't *need* a director. Of course, he needed a camera director in the control room to call the camera shots, but he had absolutely no need for any other kind of director. Jackie Gleason directed his own sketches, and I can't think of any comedy director in the business who could have done it better.

I remember an incident that happened one Saturday afternoon on the stage of Studio Fifty. Gleason was standing on the front of the stage, having an argument with his producer, his associate producer, and two CBS minor executives. I forget exactly what the argument was about, but it had something to do with a Reggie Van Gleason sketch. He permitted them to voice their opinion for about ten minutes, then he lost his patience, and indulged his Irish temper. His tirade drove them out of their seats in the orchestra, and the rich eloquence of his profanity forced them into a slow retreat up the aisle of the theater. Finally, he dismissed them with a few remarks that I've always remembered. "You know what I'd like to know?" he asked them. "I'd like to know how I succeeded in getting where I am without you jokers. While I was learning how to be funny in broken-down night clubs, where were you guys learning those dumb opinions that you pass off as pearls of wisdom? How I ever made it without you, I'll never know."

He was right. Gleason knew more about his own brand of comedy than anyone in the world. He had worked years to perfect his craft, and now that he was at the peak of his career, why should he place his future in the hands of men who thought that The Three Stooges were the ultimate in humor?

And that is why Frankenstein was an excellent choice to direct the show. The monster had no pretensions about being a director. He did exactly what Gleason told him to do, and he trusted his elves to help him get the show on the air.

The first thing I learned about Gleason was his very strong likes and dislikes. For instance, he had a soft spot for out-of-work performers. Two or three times a year he would plan a show that included a crowd scene of some kind. It might have been a scene in a village square, or a street scene in a Poor Soul sketch, or a party scene in a Reggie Van Gleason sketch. He used these crowd scenes as an excuse to hire every unemployed performer he could find. During some of these crowd scenes, I recognized old night club comics I had seen years ago, former chorus girls who were now in their fifties, and several old gents who used to be big in burlesque. Most of the people working on the show felt they understood why Gleason planned these crowd scenes. They thought that it was a nice gesture on his part to give these old-timers a few bucks once in a while. I think they missed the point. What Jackie was doing for these people was much more important than the small amount of money they received. He was giving them a chance to be back in show business. For two or three nights a year, these people could smell the greasepaint again, feel the heat of the lights and the warmth of the audience. It was very important to them.

Although Gleason had an affection for anyone who worked in back of the footlights, he was frequently disdainful toward the people who worked in front of the footlights. His suspicions about variety show producers, directors, and network executives were well founded on reality. However, some of his other negative attitudes were a little self-destructive.

For example, I got the feeling that he was conducting his own private war against the technical side of television. During the two seasons I worked on the show, I witnessed many outbursts that indicated Jackie's distaste for such things as cameras, mike booms, and technical equipment.

One Saturday while he was walking through a Poor Soul sketch, this attitude came to a head. He stopped the rehearsal, and asked the technical crew to assemble on stage. It was obvious that he was frustrated about something. Not angry, but very upset.

He started out in a low, conversational tone. "Look, guys, I want to ask you a question. . . . Now, I know you have your job to do, and I have my job to do, and all that stuff. But, I still want to ask you a question . . . in fact, a couple of questions. . . . This is a theater, right? . . . It's got a stage, and twelve or thirteen hundred seats, right? . . . The people who sit in those seats are called an audience, right?" His voice shifted gears. Now, it was lace-curtain Irish trying to prove a point in the corner bar. "This live audience is very important to me. . . . I play to this live audience. The whole show is designed for a live audience, right?" His voice shifted another gear. "Now, what I want to know is, when I'm on stage doing a sketch, why can't I see the audience, and why can't the audience see me? . . . When I look at the audience, all I see is cameras, mike booms, electrical cables, and you guys running all over the place! . . . And all the audience can see is your rear ends!"

He had a point. And the point was brought up many times during the two years I worked on the show. There were attempts to solve the problem, but nothing seemed to work. I remember Gleason's month-long war against the mike booms. Someone had told him about the new radio mikes that could be strapped on an actor's body. (They were new in those days.) These wireless microphones were completely self-contained, and eliminated the need for bulky mike booms. Gleason argued with the technical brains for a month before they finally gave up and agreed to give it a try.

On the day of the big test, the radio mikes were strapped on Gleason, Art Carney, and Audrey Meadows. Everyone else on the staff crowded into the audio room to hear the results. Gleason was cued to start talking, the audio man opened the mike, and the results were frightening. Instead of Gleason's voice, we heard a noise that sounded like a space ship trying to land in a living room.

"Humph," said the audio man. "Sounds like interference of some kind." He twisted a couple of dials, and we heard something different. It was the sound of a Model T Ford on a cold winter day.

"That's interference, all right," said the audio man. "Sounds like someone is using a small electric motor somewhere in the vicinity . . . a vacuum cleaner, or something like that. Ask Jackie to move to another part of the stage."

Gleason moved to another part of the stage, the audio man twisted the dials, and we heard twelve hundred fingernails scraping on a blackboard.

"No doubt about it. . . . We're getting interference," said the audio man. "Let's look around, and see if we can find what it is. It's a small electric motor of some kind. Like I said, a vacuum cleaner, a paint sprayer, something like that."

The search went on for more than an hour. Stagehands, June Taylor dancers, actors, two cops, and somebody's mother joined in the search for the offending "small electric motor of some kind."

Finally, one of the policemen said, "Wait a minute! I just had an idea! Follow me!" He went out the stage door to the sidewalk, with the entire Gleason show trooping after him. We followed him about ten feet up the street, where he stopped and pointed to a huge door in the next building. On the door were the words "Sub Station." We peered in a small window covered with iron bars and beheld an electric dynamo the size of a railroad car. It was a Con Edison power station, and that monster was sitting only ten feet away from Studio Fifty's backstage wall.

That finished Jackie's war against the mike booms. He ended up thinking the whole thing was pretty funny, and his only comment was, "That's the biggest goddamn vacuum cleaner I've ever seen."

The three most important ingredients of "The Jackie Gleason Show" were Jackie himself, Art Carney, and Audrey Meadows. Next to them, the three most important ingredients were the ramp, the Short Tongue Fearless camera, and a fifty-millimeter wide-angle lens.

A long narrow ramp extended from the front of the stage into the audience for about fifty feet. The camera that operated on this ramp was called a "Short Tongue Fearless." It was mounted on a steel platform which was about three-and-a-half feet wide, and six feet long. There were two fixed wheels on the front of the platform, and two movable wheels in the back that could be steered. Rising up from the platform was the "tongue," which was simply a seven-foot steel beam connected to a sort of swivel joint, so that the tongue could move from side to side, and up and down. The camera was mounted on the end of the tongue, and there was a little seat right behind the camera for the cameraman.

It took three men to operate this contraption. One very strong man to push and pull all of this metal. One semi-strong man to move the tongue from side to side, and up and down. And one very talented cameraman who could communicate what he wanted to the muscle men.

On the Gleason show, we had one of the best cameramen in the business working this camera. His name was Pat Mc-Bride, and I'll tell you more about him later on. I don't remember the name of the semi-strong tongue man, but we had *the* strongest man in television doing the pushing and pulling. His name was Casey, and I always believed that if the wheels had fallen off that steel platform, Casey would have carried it.

We would flood the stage with double the amount of light that was needed, then the fifty-millimeter lens was stopped down to F6, or F8. If you know anything about photography, you know that this combination gave the wide-angle lens a tremendous depth of focus. Casey could zip that camera up and down the ramp as fast as we wanted, and it was almost impossible to go out of focus. *Any* action on the stage could be covered, as long as we had a little bit of warning. (And, many times, without any warning at all.) Without this secret ingredient, the Gleason show would never have gotten on the air as smoothly as it did. (Remember, this was in the early fifties, when the ten-to-one Zoomar lens was a tool of the future. Most of the variety shows you see today use the ten-to-one Zoomar lens on all three cameras. By the simple turning of a handle, a cameraman can go from a wide-angle shot to a tight head shot.)

About ten every Saturday morning we would have a camera run-through with the June Taylor dancers. This was always a pleasure for the technical crew, because the numbers were always well rehearsed before they came into the studio, and the dancers knew exactly what they were doing. Personally, it was the only part of the day I actually enjoyed. I was a big fan of June Taylor, who I felt was doing her best to revive tap dancing. During the fifties, the June Taylor dancers and the Rockettes at Radio City were the only dance groups who practiced the art of foot percussion. June Taylor was the Lawrence Welk of dancing, and I thought she was on the right track.

During these rehearsals, it was my job as AD to write down the camera shots that June wanted for her dance numbers. As usual, Frankenstein resisted the information, and hoped for the best. As a former dancer, I could count bars of music without even thinking about it, and luckily, Bob Daily, the technical director, could do the same thing. During the air show, Bob and I fought a battle with Frankenstein to make sure he didn't take the right shot at the wrong time.

The ad agency people came in at noon, and we would rehearse the live commercials. Yes, we did *live* commercials in between the sketches and musical numbers. Why the sponsors trusted us to do the commercials live was always a mystery to me, because the possibilities for error were enormous.

The rest of our afternoon's work was determined by what time Jackie arrived at the theater. This arrival time varied from week to week, according to the sketches planned and his mood. If he was doing a sketch that required cues for the stagehands, or one where the humor depended on the perfect timing of something mechanical, then you knew Jackie would arrive early.

For instance—the famous Poor Soul sketch in the bakery. This was a masterpiece of sketch-level comedy, and the whole thing was based on timing. If you're old enough, you'll have no trouble remembering this classic. Gleason, playing the Poor Soul character, gets a job in a bakery. Cakes come at him on a conveyor belt and his job is to frost and cover them with whipped cream, put them in a box, and then deposit them on the shelves lining the bake shop walls.

The whole sketch depended on the speed of the conveyor belt, and the timing of the stagehand who was putting the cakes on the belt. If Gleason was doing this type of sketch he would show up at high noon, raring to go. When the sketches had no mechanical problems, he seemed to have little interest in camera rehearsals, or in any other kind of rehearsal.

When I say that the sketches weren't rehearsed, I'm talking about camera and technical rehearsals in the theater. Gleason always knew exactly what he was going to do when he arrived on Saturday. I know that the Honeymooners sketches were rehearsed in Jackie's penthouse apartment at the Park Central Hotel. I don't know how *much* they rehearsed, but I always had the feeling that they didn't spend too much time at it. This feeling wasn't based on the results, because when Gleason, Art Carney, and Audrey Meadows performed on the air, they were fantastic. My guess that the Park Central rehearsals were kept to a minimum was based on what I knew about these three people.

In the first place, Jackie Gleason and Art Carney are two of the greatest comedy actors in the world. Audrey Meadows is not in their league, but the effort she put in trying to keep up with these giants turned her into an expert. The three of them

"They trusted each other."

trusted their intuition when they performed on the air, and they trusted each other. During my two years with the show, I was the one person in the theater who knew the extent of their trust in each other's talent, because I was the only one trying to follow the script. According to Frankenstein, it was my job to stay ahead of the action, and warn everyone what was going to happen next. The monster didn't use a script, because it "cluttered up his mind."

A typical few minutes in the control room during a Honeymooners sketch went something like this:

ME:

(Eyes on script) "Everything's fine! They're sticking right to the script! . . . Pat! [the cameraman on the ramp camera] Pull a little wider. Audrey's going to make a move to the bedroom door."

PAT:

"*When* is Audrey going to the bedroom door?"

ME:

"She just did it!"

PAT:

"Aw, c'mon, Ken! . . . I almost missed it!"

ME:

"Oh, oh, Pat, I've lost them. . . . They've gone out of sequence! . . . They're not saying the dialogue I've got on this page!"

PAT:

"Try another page."

ME:

"What the hell do you think I'm doing? Do you think I *always* read this fast? . . . Wait a minute! Here we go. . . . I've found them! . . . They skipped to page eight."

PAT:

"Thanks a lot, Whelan. . . . Is it a good-looking page? . . . For God's sake, give me some information, will ya!" (It was at times like this that I got the feeling I mentioned before. The feeling that Gleason, Art, and Audrey didn't spend *too* much time rehearsing in Gleason's penthouse.)

ME:

"Watch it, Pat! . . . Gleason's going to do the pain bit! . . . Follow Carney and Gleason to the icebox. . . . Carney will close the icebox on Gleason's finger. . . . Then carry them back to the table for the pain bit." (The round kitchen table that you saw in the Honeymooners sketch was the most important prop in television. It was our insurance policy. All action scenes involving the three characters were performed at that table. Whenever they got in trouble, they headed for the table like bird dogs. The reason was simple. If they were close together, around the kitchen table, they were easier to cover with the cameras.)

ME:

"Hold it! . . . Hold it! . . . They've gone back to page six! . . . Pull back, Pat! . . . They're going to spread all over the place! . . . Get back, Pat! . . . Go wide! . . . Go wide!"

No matter how much rehearsing was done in Gleason's penthouse, and no matter how much rehearsing was done on camera, there were certain things that were bound to happen on air. They were human mistakes, but they could have been made only during the days of live television. In later years, when Gleason's shows were done on videotape, these errors were erased and the scene was done over again.

For instance, I remember one Saturday night when Gleason made an exit through the Honeymooners' bedroom door, and forgot to come back.

Gleason went through the bedroom door, followed later by Audrey Meadows. According to the script, Audrey was supposed to return with Gleason, immediately. According to Eddie Brinkman, the stage manager, Audrey couldn't *find* Gleason when she went through the bedroom door. Being a little confused, and thinking he had a little more time, he had gone looking for a Kleenex to mop his sweating brow.

As a result, *no one* came back through that bedroom door, and Art Carney was left all alone on the stage. Now remember, this was live television. Millions of people were watching, and that ramp camera had nothing else to shoot but Art Carney. He was alone, and those millions of people expected him to do something funny.

Carney could have done many things. He could have looked at the camera, imagined all the people watching him, gulped and headed for the nearest bar. He could have become frozen with fright. He could have apologized to the viewers, explaining the situation, and asking them to understand. He didn't do any of these things. Instead, he wandered over to the icebox that was a permanent prop in the Honeymooners set. He made a funny bit out of looking through the icebox for something to eat.

We were holding our breath in the control room. The stage manager was running around backstage trying to find Gleason while Carney continued to bluff it out on stage. By some miracle of good luck, Art found an orange in the icebox, and for the next two minutes he sat at the kitchen table and peeled that orange. That's all he did, so help me God. He didn't say a word. He just sat there in front of millions of people, and peeled an orange. Of course, it was the funniest two minutes I've ever seen, but that's not important. What stunned me was the complete trust this man had in his own talent. He never faltered for a split second, and I doubt if anyone watching the show at home was aware that anything was wrong.

Jackie and Audrey made their entrance through the bedroom door before Art finished peeling the orange, but I was convinced that if they hadn't shown up when they did, Carney could have gone on for hours thinking of funny things to do.

Incidentally, that's the only cue I remember Gleason missing during the two years I worked on the show. It wasn't because he was such a hard worker, or that he rehearsed himself to death. (I always believed that he was basically lazy.) Gleason has a photographic memory. He could memorize an entire Honeymooners sketch in one hour, and be letter perfect three days later when he went on the air.

One of the funniest mishaps we had on the Gleason show happened during a Reggie Van Gleason sketch that had been rehearsed very carefully. If you remember any of those sketches, you'll also remember the little toy electric train that delivered shots of whiskey to Reggie. About five feet of track extended into Reggie's apartment, leading from a hole in the right wall. When Gleason pushed a button, the little train would come through the hole in the wall, chug down the track, and stop with a toot of its whistle. On one of the flatcars would be a shot of booze which Gleason would down with a flourish. Then he would press another button, and the train would carry the empty shot glass back through the hole.

In this particular sketch, Reggie made a paper airplane out of a piece of stationery, opened a window on the right wall of the apartment, threw the airplane out the window, and closed the window. Then he walked over to his booze train, and went through the ritual of getting a drink. When the train had disappeared through the hole in the wall with the empty shot glass, Reggie made a big show of looking at his wrist watch to check the time. Then he walked to the window on the *left* wall of the apartment, opened it, and the paper airplane would fly in through the window. Of course, the airplane flew in through the window because a stagehand threw it in. The stagehand was hidden behind the downstage side of the window frame so that he wouldn't be seen in the camera shot, or by the audience. Everything went fine during rehearsal, because the routine was fairly simple. But, when we did the sketch on the air, this is what happened.

Gleason made his paper airplane. . . . He threw it out the window on the right. He walked down to his train, and had his drink. . . . He looked at his watch. . . . Then he walked over to the window on the left, to watch his airplane come sailing into the room.

When he got to the window, there was an eighty-two-year-old stagehand standing outside the window in full view of the audience. In his uplifted hand he held a paper airplane. The audience roared with laughter, not knowing whether it was part of the sketch, or an accident. Gleason just stood there, staring at the stagehand in disbelief. When the audience's laughter subsided, Gleason opened the window, and said to the stagehand, "Well, as long as you're there, you might as well throw it." The stagehand threw the airplane in through the window, and then, having done his job, he shrugged his shoulders and walked out of sight. Gleason received a round of applause for his quick thinking.

(The explanation for the mistake was very simple. The stagehand who had rehearsed the bit became suddenly ill just before the show went on the air. The stage manager picked the first stagehand he could find as a substitute for the airplane throwing. He either picked the wrong stagehand, or he didn't have time to rehearse the old guy. In any case, the result was another classic goof that could only happen during the days of live television.)

Well, that's enough about the Gleason show. I'd rather not talk about it anymore.

Gleason himself? Well, as I said before, I hardly knew him. If I met him tomorrow he wouldn't remember me, anymore than he'd remember the guy that shined his shoes in Boston in 1945. I doubt if he would know Bob Daily if he bumped into him. It has nothing to do with Gleason's being a nice guy or a bad guy. It's just that Bob and I did *our* thing in the control room, and Jackie did *his* thing on the stage. We were the elves, and very few people want to admit that they owe anything to elves.

Personally, I liked Gleason. In many ways, Jackie was like any other Irishman you might bump into. He liked to argue about things, and I doubt that he cared what side he was on. He liked his booze, but he definitely was not a drunk. He liked to be the boss, but all Irishmen want to be the boss. Actually, I think that Jackie Gleason was born to be a cop and he missed the boat because he was much too fat, and much too talented.

I'm glad that he didn't end up on the police force, because he gave some wonderful Saturday nights to millions of people.

He didn't give *me* any wonderful Saturday nights . . . but what the hell!

CHAPTER 7

"The Ed Sullivan Show"

The following season, in addition to being associate director on the Gleason show, I was assigned to "The Ed Sullivan Show." The Gleason show aired on Saturday night, and the Sullivan show aired on Sunday night. It guaranteed me a fun-packed weekend.

I realized later that without my experience on the Gleason show, the Sullivan show would have been the end of my television career. I know that if I had been assigned the Sullivan show one year earlier, I wouldn't have lived through the first Sunday night.

Compared to "The Ed Sullivan Show," the Gleason show

was a well-organized group of perfectionists who rehearsed too much.

There was only one person connected with "The Ed Sullivan Show" who knew what was going on, and that person was Ed Sullivan . . . and he wasn't telling.

In 1953, the producer of the show was Marlo Lewis, who dressed very well. I don't know what kind of producer he was, because I don't think Sullivan told *him* what was happening.

The director of the show was Johnny Wray (not the singer). He was an ex-choreographer with years of Broadway experience behind him. I found him to be a talented guy and a nice guy, which were the two worst qualities you could have for this type of show.

Of course, I'm exaggerating when I say that Sullivan was the only one who knew what was going on. There must have been some kind of planning during the week, because the scenery always arrived on time, and sometimes Ray Bloch had the correct music. Yes, I'm convinced that there was some sort of communication among the production staff prior to Sunday, but on Sunday morning all communication stopped dead.

I usually spent the first hour trying to get someone to give me a run down sheet for the show. A run down sheet was simply the listing of the various acts and commercials in order of their appearance. There was no script of course, because it was a big vaudeville show. When I finally got hold of my run down sheet, the next hour was spent in trying to find out if I had an *up-to-date* run down. Changes were being made every five minutes.

"Hey, Marlo. Can I look at your run down?" I'd ask.

"Why do you want to look at my run down? You've got one of your own."

"I just want to check if I have an *up-to-date* run down."

"What color paper is your run down sheet, Whelan?"

"Yellow, sir," I'd answer. "My run down sheet is yellow."

"Yellow paper? That's ridiculous, Whelan. You're goofing off. That was last Thursday's run down sheet . . . It's obsolete."

Marlo would then walk in the general direction of Ed Sullivan, hoping that Ed would talk to him about the new changes.

I would run to the stage manager, Eddie Brinkman.

"Eddie, what color is your run down sheet?"

"Light green . . . what color have you got?"

"Yellow . . . Marlo says it's obsolete."

"He's right, you're three days behind. Get with it, Whelan."

"Do you think you've got the right one, Eddie?"

"I don't know. Last week the magic color was pink. Why don't we check with Sullivan's chauffeur. He's very reliable."

About three o'clock Sunday afternoon, I would meet the right person with the right run down sheet, but that was only the opening skirmish. The battle of the run down continued with penciled changes being made every ten minutes. They used pencil because they did a lot of erasing.

About five o'clock it would start to get desperate.

"Marlo, who does Tony Martin follow? I've got him following the West Point Glee Club."

"For God's sake, Whelan! What's the matter with you? That was changed twenty minutes ago. Tony Martin follows Alice and Her Birds."

"That's not what Mr. Sullivan says."

"How do you know what Ed says? Have you been bothering him again with your idiotic questions?"

"I didn't bother him, sir. I overheard Tony Martin telling Mr. Sullivan that he refused to follow birds, and Mr. Sullivan said that Mr. Martin was right. Then Mr. Sullivan said that

Mr. Martin would follow the West Point Glee Club."

We were both wrong. Tony Martin ended up following a ventriloquist.

The desperate search for information continued right up to fifteen minutes before we went on the air. The show, as you well know, aired at eight o'clock Sunday night. At twenty minutes to eight we were all summoned to a final meeting in Ed Sullivan's dressing room. The group consisted of Johnny Wray, the director; Eddie Brinkman, the stage manager; Marlo Lewis, the producer; and me. The five of us would sit in the dressing room, nervously comparing run down sheets while Ed Sullivan shaved. It was important that our run down sheets matched, because we all knew that in the next five minutes we were going to get more changes.

We waited for the voice from the bathroom.

"Marlo, let's put the Indian Sun Dance Ceremony right after the circus bit."

"Great idea," said Marlo.

"There's no problem there, Eddie . . . right?" asked the voice from the bathroom. "There's a one-minute commercial in between. You can handle it, Eddie, right?"

Eddie the stage manager began to resemble a heart attack victim. His breathing would become labored, his eyes would roll upwards, and his face would suddenly develop varicose veins that didn't exist on weekdays.

Eddie's outer voice would say, "Right, Mr. Sullivan. No problem."

Eddie's inner voice would say, "Oh, Jesus Christ! Have I got a problem! During that one-minute commercial, I'll have to get rid of three elephants, a circus ring, ten fake tent poles, and one Bavarian elephant trainer who doesn't speak English. No problem at all, Mr. Sullivan. It will leave me plenty of time to set the four teepees, fly in the desert back drop, spread the imitation sand on the stage, and get twenty Indians on stage . . . No problem at all, Mr. Sullivan!"

The voice from the bathroom again. "Is the AD here?"

"Yes, sir," I'd answer. "Right here."

"Good. That film clip from the John Wayne movie is too long."

"Two minutes and twenty-six seconds, sir." I was trying to be valuable.

"Right, it's too long. I want to cut out of it when the wagon wheels show up."

"Wagon wheels, right! . . . Wagon wheels?"

Voice from the bathroom. "Some place in there I saw a close-up of wagon wheels."

"Cut out with the wagon wheels . . . right!"

The sound of water running in the bathroom, and more instructions. ". . . And Marlo, would you tell Ray Bloch to cut Tony Martin's musical introduction down to eight bars."

"That's what he's playing, Ed, eight bars." Marlo would adjust his cuff links.

"Then cut it to four bars. It sounds as if we're introducing the Pope."

And so it would go on. At fifteen minutes before air time we were released for active duty. From that moment until eight o'clock, speed was the important thing.

The stage manager had twelve minutes to work out the logistics of the change with twenty-three members of a very strong union—the stagehands. If they didn't hit Eddie with a stage weight, he would then try to communicate the change to the Bavarian elephant trainer who didn't speak English. If he was lucky, he'd have thirty seconds to conquer the Indians.

My mission was simpler than Eddie's, but the enemy was the same, the clock. I had to find the Teleprompter operator, and make the changes on the Teleprompter machine. (In those days, the cueing device mounted on the camera was owned by the Teleprompter Company.) After the constant changes during the day, the roll of script on the Teleprompter machine looked like shredded cabbage. Every time we made a change the script had to be cut up and taped back together again.

If it was a *good* Sunday, I would have time after the frantic cutting and taping to dash up to the control room and tell the technical director about the wagon wheels.

The director spent the twelve minutes trying to get the technical crew up to date.

Marlo, the producer, might have had the hardest job. He had to convince another strong union that they should cut four bars out of Tony Martin's music intro.

It may sound as if we spent the entire day trying to keep up with the changes in the run down. This was not true. We also rehearsed a few things. Not many things, but a few.

All of the singing acts were rehearsed. It was usually a music rehearsal with Ray Bloch . . . no camera rehearsal. If Johnny Wray had staged some special choreography to back up the vocalist, then we would rehearse it on camera. If we had a ballet company on the show, we would have a camera rehearsal, and the dramatic scenes from Broadway shows were always rehearsed on camera. I'd say that about fifty percent of the show was rehearsed in front of the cameras, the rest of the acts were "winged." Without a camera rehearsal, the camera crew had no more information about what was going to happen next than the viewer sitting at home. I found that most of the men who were adept at "winging" were deeply religious. (In fact, I've always believed that the term "winged" came from the old World War II song, "Coming in on a Wing and a Prayer.")

All of this may strike you as a rather shipshod way to put on a top-rated network television show, and you're right, but it was the only way it could be done in the time allotted for rehearsal. The two devils of live TV were time and budget. Those two factors cut a few years off the lives of a great many men, disrupted marriages, rendered sexual tigers impotent, and gladdened the hearts of the American Distillers' Association.

CHAPTER 8

On the
Air with
Ed Sullivan

In 1953, the actual experience of putting a live Ed Sullivan
show on the air was like having an orgasm, but not half the
fun.

A few months ago I ran into Bob Daily, one of two technical directors I worked with on the Gleason and Sullivan
shows. He's now a sports director at CBS. He was a great TD
in the early days, and he probably is just as great a sports
director. We had a drink together, reminiscing about the good
old days. This conversation took place *seventeen years* after we
had worked together, yet, when we got to talking about the live
Ed Sullivan shows, his drinking tempo picked up, and his voice

83

changed. And Bob was one of the strong ones. It was like that. It was crazy.

On one particular Sunday night in 1953, Ed did a two-minute introduction to Peggy Lee. The lights dimmed, the spotlight appeared on the curtain, the curtain opened, and the stage was empty.

Camera two had the opening shot on Peggy's first song. The cameraman was Pat McBride, the talented cameraman who always knew what he was doing. He dollied in for a loose waist shot, and then he suddenly stopped moving in. His voice came over our head sets.

"I don't see any Peggy Lee. Do you guys see Peggy Lee?"

"No, Pat," answered the director, "we don't see any Peggy Lee."

Marlo yelled into Ray Bloch's mike, "Repeat the music intro, Ray! We can't find Peggy Lee!"

Across the theater I could see Ray Bloch look toward the glass-enclosed control room. His lips mouthed the words, "No shit!" Ray repeated the music intro four times while Pat panned his camera all over the stage, searching for Peggy Lee.

Suddenly, Johnny Wray screamed, "Up, Pat! Pan up!"

Pat obeyed the director and ended up with a shot of a guy sitting on a trapeze. Pat asked calmly, "What's Peggy Lee doing up there?"

"It's not Peggy Lee, Pat! It's the Flying Montoyas!"

"Never heard of them," said Pat.

"Do the best you can, Pat! It's a trapeze act!"

As Ray Bloch switched into the Flying Montoyas' music, Pat said, "I figured that out already."

Incidentally, this mishap occurred because Eddie Brinkman was out with the flue, and we had a substitute stage manager who did not know about the mysteries of the run down sheet.

" . . . and here is Peggy Lee!" (Or somebody!)

On another Sunday night, we had the U.S. Army's champion drill team on the show. It was a black drill team from one of the southern Army camps. No one was bothered by the lack of a camera rehearsal, because we were experts at this sort of thing. The Sullivan show had a soft spot for any group of people who could keep in step with each other. We had marchers on the show every other week. Our favorite marching people were the West Pointers, who proved that the ability to march in unison was a major factor in the defense of America. Using this premise, the Rockettes at the Radio City Music Hall were the greatest threat to Communism in the Western Hemisphere. If fifty gout victims had learned to limp in unison, they would have been on the Sullivan show five times a year.

With this kind of experience behind us, we were confident that we could handle the champion drill team without a camera rehearsal. At eight twenty that Sunday night, the curtains opened, the team drilled with great style, and we got the right shots with no trouble at all. Suddenly, the marchers formed a column of four abreast, and headed straight for camera two. Now, this may not sound unusual or frightening to *you*, but for two reasons it became a harrowing experience for the cameraman on camera two. First, camera two operated on a five-foot-wide ramp that extended into the audience from the stage. The second reason was that the cameraman was new and inexperienced.

When the column of black soldiers began marching down the ramp, there was only one thing that the cameraman could do, and that was "retreat." They kept coming at him, doing a crazy manual of arms with their rifles, and he continued to retreat. I looked out the control room window, and saw the cameraman glancing over his shoulder to see how much ramp he had left. We could hear his muttered remarks over the head sets. "What the hell are they doing? Are they crazy?"

"Pull back, Jimmy!" yelled the director. "Pull back!"

Between terrified looks over his shoulder, and even more terrified looks into his camera view finder, Jimmy found time to say, "You've got a steel trap mind, Johnny! Where the hell else can I go?"

With about six feet of ramp behind him, Jimmy turned paranoid. "They're after me! They're after me!" With two feet of ramp behind him, he ripped off his head set, jumped off the end of the ramp, and ran into the lobby of the theater. The sergeant in charge of the drill team barked a command, the soldiers did an about face toward the stage, and we finished in fine style . . . minus camera two.

A similar thing happened on another occasion. José Greco, the famous Spanish dancer, was booked on the show with his full company of dancers. As usual, we didn't get a full camera rehearsal, but this time it wasn't the show's lack of rehearsal time that caused the mishap, it was Mr. Greco.

In the middle of rehearsal, one of his male dancers fouled up a complicated bit of Spanish heel work. José responded with a tirade of abusive language that was not Spanish. (It was English with a Brooklyn accent.) This scene broke up the rehearsal, and led to the rather bizarre event that happened when we went on the air.

During the performance, we got through the rehearsed part of the act with no trouble at all, and were winging the unrehearsed part fairly well. Then it happened. The cameraman involved was George Moses, on camera two. George was a great cameraman with a great sense of humor. Toward the end of the unrehearsed dance number, José began a fantastic display of flamenco heel work. At the time, George was on a wide-angle fifty-millimeter lens with a cover shot of the whole group. Cameras one and three were too far away to grab a tight shot of Greco's feet, so the director yelled, "Go ahead in, George! Push right in there, George . . . a tight shot of his feet!"

George dollied his camera in and got a tight shot of the flashing heels. Now, if you know anything about cameras, you know that in order to get a tight shot with a fifty-millimeter lens you have to get very close to the subject. George was about two feet away from Greco's demented heels, in the middle of the stage, surrounded by a gang of crazy Spanish dancers. Greco's feet pounded the stage floor like two sadistic madmen. The mike boom moved in and dipped low to pick up the machine gun sounds.

Suddenly, the crazy heels started to move toward George's camera. George pulled his camera back a few inches. "Stay tight, George," ordered the director. "Stay tight."

Greco's feet moved toward George again, but George did not move back. He was staying tight on orders from the director. Then we all heard Greco's voice say, "Move back! I'm coming down stage!"

The director screamed, "Get that boom out of there! Get it out of there! That Spanish dancer is yelling at George!"

The boom moved up and away from the action, silencing Greco's heels and mouth. Looking out the control room window, we could see the battle going on between Greco and George.

Greco was obviously screaming at George to pull back his camera, but George was resisting. George's great sense of humor was matched by his stubbornness, and he didn't like a Brooklyn Spanish dancer telling him what to do. You didn't have to be a lip reader to know exactly what Greco was saying to George, because we could hear George's reactions over our intercoms: "I'm not moving an inch, you son of a bitch! Drop dead, you grease ball!"

The director tried to solve the problem by ordering George to move back, but it was a personal fight now, and George wasn't listening to direction. At one point, he started to take off his head set. It looked as if we might have a fist fight between a cameraman and a Spanish dancer . . . on network television.

"No, George! No!" yelled the technical director. "He'll kick you to death with those heels! Now, pull back. We'll straighten it out after the show."

George obeyed his TD. He started to dolly back as Greco moved forward. We all breathed easier. The crisis seemed to be over.

Then I happened to glance out the control room window. I couldn't believe what I was looking at. As George dollied back, he was mimicking Greco's brilliant heel work with some heel work of his own. Every time Greco would give out with a spectacular display of flamenco heel stomping, George would stop the camera movement and answer him a burst of foot percussion that might not have been Spanish, but it certainly was spectacular. In the control room, we all stared in disbelief. The second time George performed his little dance, the audience started to laugh. The audio man killed the audience mikes so that twenty million viewers at home wouldn't go crazy trying to figure out why an audience was laughing at a tight shot of a Spanish dancer's feet.

By the time Greco arrived at the front of the stage, he didn't seem to care about his fancy heel work. In fact it looked very much like he was trying to kick the camera.

After the show, we hustled George across town to a Chinese restaurant where we calmed him down with ten martinis, a double order of Lobster Cantonese, and some soothing dialogue.

I might add that George never capitalized on his talent as a Spanish dancer.

CHAPTER **9**

The
Seven-Day
Wonders
or
The dramatic
show director
and his woes

A few years ago, Franklin Schaffner was nominated for an Academy Award as best director of the year. The motion picture he directed that year was "Patton." A year later he received another nomination for directing "Nicholas and Alexandra." I'm sure that I received as much satisfaction from these nominations as Mr. Schaffner himself, because twenty years ago I had awarded him my own personal Oscar when he was directing "Studio One" on television.

Franklin Schaffner was the first genuine, big-time, live dramatic show director that I ever worked with. I was his associate director for exactly one show in 1951, and he immediately became my model of what a TV dramatic director should be. Later in my career, I directed my own share of soap operas, and some situation comedies, but my awe of the big boys never diminished. The big boys were men like Franklin Schaffner, who directed the one-hour, prime-time dramatic shows; Paul Nickell, Fielder Cook, Sidney Lumet, Arthur Penn, John Frankenheimer. I might have missed a few names, but it was this group of incredible men that made the Golden Age of television actually golden. They directed the "Philco Playhouse" shows, "Studio One," "Playhouse 90," etc. What they attempted and accomplished every week will never be duplicated in any form of show business.

The average feature film runs an hour and a half. If the director of a quality feature film completed the picture in four months, his company would give him a medal, fix him up with 365 starlets, and name the studio commissary after him. In *seven days,* the director of any one of the live television shows I have mentioned had to interpret the values of the script, rehearse his actors, help plan the sets with the scenic designer, work out lighting cues with the lighting director, plan his camera shots, plan his mike boom positions, and so on, and so on. Then he had to go on the air with his one-hour feature, shoot more than three hundred camera shots, and *edit* the whole thing while he was on the air.

John Frankenheimer, the director of "Playhouse 90," was a real miracle man of live TV. His actual show ran one hour and a half, which is the length of the average motion picture. "Playhouse 90" was a live show for one season, before they started putting it on videotape. During that first season, Frankenheimer directed one show that used twenty-two different scenic sets and seven television cameras. Now, try to visualize what I'm saying. He had filled one huge studio in California with *twenty-two* completely separate physical scenes. And

"One of the directors with the golden touch." (If it wasn't a comedy.)

they were not the usual run-of-the-mill interior room sets. He had exterior sets of a hotel, a lake scene with a boat house and a dock, a suburban street, one half of a real bus, a set-up for a live car crash, etc.

His script was one hundred and four pages long. The script was marked with two hundred and sixty camera shots, plus two hundred and fifty released camera cues. The lighting director had sixty-two light cues. Three sound men supplied one hundred and twenty different sound effects.

While the show was on the air, there were ninety-four people working on the studio floor. Thirty-five actors, thirty-two stagehands, twenty-five technicians, and two stage managers.

Several years after this show was aired, one of the cameramen who worked on the show told me about an incident that happened in the control room just before air time. He had come into the control room looking for a maintenance man to check out his head set. While he was talking to the other technician, he noticed Frankenheimer sitting in his director's chair, silently staring at the script in front of him. The director wasn't talking to anyone, and no one dared talk to him. As the minutes ticked by toward air time, he just sat there staring at the script. Finally, he looked up at the technical director, and said, "You know what? I have to be insane to think we're going to get through this thing." He stared at the script for another minute, and said, "We're all insane . . . we're absolutely nuts!"

The secret of directing a live dramatic show without going nuts was in doing your homework. During the five days preceding the day of the show, the director had to complete all of his planning and decision making down to the smallest detail.

The sixth day was air day. It is almost impossible to describe what the director of a one-hour live dramatic show went through on the sixth day. At seven o'clock in the morning, he walked into the studio and saw his secretary for the first time.

The rooms, hallways, and street scenes, which for five days had only existed on paper, were suddenly real. If he was a good director, he would spend a little time walking through the sets, checking to see if his planning had been accurate. While he was reviewing his technical problems, he was also thinking about other things. It might have been an acting problem. Something like how he could convince the actress playing the minister's daughter that she was giving a convincing performance of a 42nd Street hooker. Or he might have been cursing himself for allowing the producer and writer to cast a screaming faggot in the role of the truck driver lover.

Eight A.M. was ego time. This was the beginning of the first dry rehearsal. A dry rehearsal was a rehearsal for actors only, without cameras. During this first rehearsal on the actual set, the actors, suddenly realizing that the day of the show had arrived, would start to have opening night terrors. That was the deadly thing about the age of live television. Every time you did a show it was opening night. Everyone concerned had only one chance to do it right. We had relatives, bosses, and millions of strangers watching . . . and there was no place to hide your mistakes.

The opening night terrors were familiar to all of us, but they brought out the worst in actors. During this first dry rehearsal, leading men would drink quarts of Alka-Seltzer. Their voices would disappear, and throat specialists would show up with mysterious sprays and gargles. Young actresses would telephone their mothers, and famous actors would break into tears when they forgot their lines. The director would discover that none of his actors knew how to open doors, sit on sofas, or walk across a room without tripping. By 9 A.M., everyone in the studio was convinced that the whole thing was hopeless.

After this emotional dry rehearsal, the director would hold a short meeting with the cast to give them his notes on the way things were going. ("Director's notes" are the director's criticisms of the cast's work during the previous rehearsal.) The director's notes could be constructive, unconstructive, or based on sheer hate from working with certain actors for five days. It really didn't matter what the criticisms were based on, the result was the same . . . bloodshed.

The director's notes to the actors would bring the following accusations from the actors:

1. The director was an untalented shithead who should be bagging groceries in a supermarket.

2. The director was a faggot who could only relate to lesbian actresses.

3. The director was a right-wing reactionary who had missed the social implications of the script.

4. The Director's mental health was suspect.

5. The director was anti-Semitic, and hated the leading lady because her agent was Jewish.

All of this would result in:

1. A short speech by the leading lady, condemning television as a medium not worth her talent.

2. Veiled threats to punch the director in the mouth after the show.

3. Several tearful phone calls to agents, personnel managers, and lawyers.

And so on, and so on . . .

After the note-giving session, the director would begin his first rehearsal with the cameras and all the other technical facilities.

After this camera blocking rehearsal, the director would have a short meeting with the crew to give *them* his notes. The reactions to these notes were just about the same as the actors' reactions, only the language was dirtier.

There would be a short break for lunch, and then the director would attempt his first nonstop runthrough with all facilities. The nonstop attempt was a joke. There were plenty of stops, because it was during this rehearsal that everyone in the studio became a director or producer. A nineteen-year-old actress would halt the proceedings to correct a fifty-year-old acting veteran on a line reading. An overly creative cameraman might have a brilliant idea on how to restage a scene so that it could be shot on one camera. A stagehand would inform the director that the leading man's character was not logical from a psychological standpoint. (There were more directors in the stagehand union than there were in the Directors' Guild.) The cop on the beat, who had dropped in for a free cup of coffee, would have a better exit line for one of the characters. And the guy who delivered the coffee might offer a few suggestions concerning plot structure.

It was a game that everyone had to play. Every person in the studio seemed to feel that if he didn't second guess the director at least once, he didn't belong in show business.

The last rehearsal before going on the air was laughingly called a "dress rehearsal." This was supposed to be the finished product, the way the show would look on the air. I don't know about the other two networks, but at CBS, the words "dress rehearsal" would get a laugh in any studio we had. It was an inside joke. If a lighting director said to a stagehand, "Forget it, we'll fix it during dress rehearsal," the stagehand would fall on the floor with laughter. If a director said to a cameraman, "Don't worry about it, Al, we'll correct it during dress rehearsal," the cameraman might have had convulsions right on the spot. The reason for the uncontrolled laughter was simple. Dress rehearsals were a myth. They didn't exist.

I am still acquainted with hundreds of people who worked on live dramatic shows during the Golden Age, and not one of them can remember a *completed* dress rehearsal. The enemy was time. It was impossible to get through the necessary four rehearsals in one single day. At various periods during my AD ing career, I worked on all of CBS's prime-time dramatic shows. The directors were not only good, some of them were great. But with the amount of time allotted them, they all found it was impossible to put on a real dress rehearsal.

Thirty minutes after the mythical dress rehearsal, the show went on the air, ready or not. This half hour between dress rehearsal and air time were the blackest thirty minutes in a director's week. The mistakes of the day marched through his mind like a paranoid parade. The dozens of things that had gone wrong in the last rehearsal encouraged him to smoke ten cigarettes in twenty-nine minutes. It was during these few minutes before air that many directors returned to God and church.

About three minutes before air time, the control room wit would come up with his big funny of the week. He'd put his hand on the director's shoulder, and say, "Nothing to worry about, Frank . . . We always get on the air, and we always get off . . . right?"

It was at this movent that John Frankenheimer expressed the opinion, "I have to be insane to think we're going to get through this thing! . . . We're all insane . . . We're absolutely nuts!" I'm sure that every director of a live dramatic show had the same opinion many times during his career.

Twenty years later Franklin Schaffner was nominated an Oscar as best motion picture director of the year. He must have been very pleased, but I doubt if he was surprised. He was a big winner a long time ago . . . when he was a nut.

CHAPTER 10

Short Tales from the Golden Age

As I mentioned before, most of the incidents that sound funny when I retell them were not funny at all when they actually happened. They were mistakes. Sometimes these mistakes resulted in a person losing his job, or being banished to a limbo assignment that buried him for several years. Sometimes the mistake ruined a show and the sponsor would demand his money back. And sometimes the mistake resulted in physical injury.

For instance, there's a story I've been telling for years that always gets a laugh, yet, in the punch line to the story, a good cameraman breaks his leg.

101

When I tell the story, I always say that it happened on the Garry Moore daytime show, in the early fifties. I remember it that way, so that's the way I tell it. If I've got the wrong show, it doesn't matter. I was there, and it actually happened.

The incident happened to a very talented cameraman who was assigned to work on a mike boom, because of the sudden illness of the regular mike boom man. The illness was caused by his consuming sixteen legitimate martinis at the neighborhood pub. The very talented cameraman hadn't worked on a mike boom for three years, and before I tell you why this piece of information is important, let me tell you what a mike boom looked like.

A mike boom was a long metal arm with a microphone attached to its end. The man who operated the boom worked on a platform five feet above the floor. The platform was mounted on three wheels so that it could be pushed around.

We were in the middle of rehearsal when a phone call came in for this cameraman who was subbing for the regular boom man. Someone opened the control room door and yelled at the guy to come to the phone. The man took off his head set. Then, forgetting that he wasn't standing on the floor, he walked off the five foot platform and broke his leg.

When it happened, we thought that he had only sprained his ankle, so we all laughed like hell . . . which makes this one of the few funny stories that were funny when they happened.

As long as we're talking about mike booms, here's a little gem that I *know* happened on the Garry Moore daytime show, because I got blamed for it. It occurred during a two-week period that Clarence Schimmel, the regular director, was on vacation. Because I knew the show very well, I was upgraded from associate director to director for these two weeks.

One day we had a ventriloquist on the show. On the same day we had an inexperienced man working the mike boom. We found out later that the man had spent his first two years at CBS buried in the film projection room, being paroled from the dungeon only two days prior to the incident. As usual, we spent so much time rehearsing the live commercials, we never got around to rehearsing the ventriloquist, and when the guy started his act on the air show, we knew we *should* have rehearsed it.

The ventriloquist began his routine, and within twenty seconds, we knew that something was terribly wrong with the audio. When the ventriloquist spoke in his own voice we could hear him fine, but when he spoke in the dummy's voice we couldn't hear a word he said. This strange phenomenon went on for a full minute, while the audio man went out of his mind trying to find the trouble.

Suddenly, the audio man let out a yell. "Oh, no! . . . Oh, no! . . . I don't believe it! . . . I know exactly what's wrong, but I don't believe it!" Then he jumped up from his seat, and ran out the control room door. Fifteen seconds later, the dummy's voice cleared up, and the audio went back to normal.

When the show was over, I asked the audio man what the trouble had been.

"Very simple," he said. "Every time the dummy said something, the guy on the boom was taking the mike away from the ventriloquist, and pointing it toward the dummy. . . . Think about it for a minute, it's very subtle."

One very macabre story that I tell involves the stagehand union. You'll remember, from my experience with the swimming pool on "The Garry Moore Show," that they are a very tightly departmentalized union. The electrical department will not handle a prop. The prop department will not go within ten feet of a lighting board. The number one carpenter wouldn't consider driving a nail into anything but scenery. Of course, there were times when the stagehands' departmental neurosis could be irritating, or even funny in a morbid way. One of the great stagehand stories happened on a daytime interview show during the late fifties. An old-time comic had a heart attack and died while being interviewed on the show. The producer telephoned the police, and the director told the stagehands to remove the body. During the commercial break, the stagehands became involved in a history-making dispute. The electricians wouldn't touch the body. The carpenters were horrified at the very thought of corpse-handling being included in their duties. The property department suddenly decided they should all go out for coffee. At the end of the two-minute commercial break, the show went on, with the host interviewing a new guest sitting in a chair to the right of him, and the poor dead old comic slumped in a chair to the left of him. The camera shots did not include the dead man, naturally. While the show continued, the stagehands made a hurried phone call to the head of their union local, the omnipotent Mr. Yaeger. They told him about their problem, and awaited his pronouncement.

STAGEHAND:

> "Yeah, the guy's dead. . . . They want us to move him. . . . Well, we don't know what to do. . . . The situation has never come up before!"

YAEGER:

> "So what's the big deal? . . . Move the son of a bitch!"

STAGEHAND:

> "What department moves him?"

YAEGER:

"Well, it certainly hasn't got anything to do with the electrical department. . . . And you can't call a corpse a piece of scenery, right?"

STAGEHAND:

"Right, it can't be scenery, the body isn't attached to the floor. . . ."

YAEGER:

"Then he's a prop. . . . The property department moves him."

STAGEHAND:

"A dead guy is a prop? Since when?"

YAEGER:

"Since right now!"

And that was the birth of another departmental rule in Local One of the stagehand union.

There is one short story about live television that was a legend for years. I was not an eyewitness to this incident, but I heard the story from so many people, I think I can vouch for its authenticity. It all happened on a show called "Man Against Crime." I'm not going to tell you who the "Man" was, because he's a fine actor, and the incident might embarrass him. If you remember who starred in "Man Against Crime," that's fine. If you don't remember, the story is still funny.

"Man Against Crime" was a detective story show. The detective uncovered the clues as he went along, and the home audience tried to guess the murderer before the detective did.

The final scene was typical of all detective stories. The crime fighter would gather all of the suspects into one room for a confrontation. One by one, he would eliminate the suspects, finally ending up with the real murderer. This final summing up usually sounded something like this:

"Let's start with *you,* Charlie. When you made the telephone call to Susan on that fateful night, you didn't know that Susan was the illegitimate daughter of the victim. And you didn't know that she still loved the victim, as any daughter would love her own father, even though she knew she was illegitimate. And *you,* Susan . . . you didn't realize that the man on the other end of the phone was the cab driver who drove you home, *and* your half-brother. . . . As for *you,* Richard, you really believe you're the murderer, don't you? You poisoned the victim's Corn Flakes on the morning of the polo matches. But the victim did not succumb to poisoned Corn Flakes. He was killed by a blow on the back of the head. The murder weapon was a polo pony's horseshoe! You didn't know that, Richard! . . . As for you, Bruce . . ." And so it went, until the detective finally pointed his finger at the guilty man.

One night on "Man Against Crime," the confrontation scene turned into one of the funniest mistakes ever seen on live TV. On this particular show, the detective had gathered all of the suspects into a hospital room for his summing up routine. One of the suspects was a patient in the hospital, which was a good excuse to stage the scene in a hospital room.

The patient-suspect reclined on the hospital bed, wrapped in bandages. According to the script, he had been trapped in a burning automobile, and was suffering third-degree burns. His arms, his hands, and his head were completely covered with bandages. The only communication he had with the outside world was two small eye holes cut out of the bandages.

The scene began in the usual way, with the detective identifying the various suspects assembled in the room, and in some cases, introducing the suspects to each other. This part of the scene went fine. Everything happened the way it was supposed to happen.

Then the detective went into his big, final scene, the summing up of the clues, and the naming of the murderer:

"Let's start with you, Tony. You were the one who rigged the fire bomb in Mr. Wilson's car. You *thought* that you were placing the bomb in *Mrs.* Wilson's car."

Then, the detective turned toward Mr. Wilson, the man covered with bandages. "As for you, Mr. Wilson, I happen to know that . . . I happen to know that . . . I happen to . . . I . . ."

The detective couldn't go on. His mind had gone blank, and he couldn't remember his lines. In show business, there is a term for this sort of thing, called "going up in your lines." In a theater, in front of an audience of several hundred people, going up in your lines can be terribly embarrassing. On live television, in front of an audience of several *million* people, it was spine-chilling.

The detective's face turned chalk white, his eyes became glazed, and you could see his throat muscles trying to pump a little saliva into a very dry mouth.

The actor who was playing the detective had a lot of guts. His memory had deserted him, but his mind still functioned, and he had control of his body. He ran around the hospital room, pointing his finger at all the suspects. Then he took another shot at it. He went back to the hospital bed and pointed his finger at the bandaged Mr. Wilson. "As for you, Mr. Wilson . . . I happen to know that . . . I happen to . . ." All of this action took exactly thirteen seconds. Thirteen seconds as long as a week in Philadelphia.

The people in the control room were frozen with panic. The director managed to keep his head, and realized that the camera shot on the air was a single shot of the finger-waving detective. He quickly put another camera on the air, with a wider shot that included most of the other actors in the scene. The director was praying that one of the actors would do something to help . . . anything!

His prayers were answered. One of the actors started to prompt the detective with the next line of dialogue. Unfortunately, the actor who was trying to help the detective was the very man that the detective was accusing—the much-bandaged Mr. Wilson.

If you were a home viewer, it was a very funny situation. If you were involved with the show, it was death in the early evening.

When Mr. Wilson tried to feed the detective his next line, the bandages covering his mouth fluttered like a female cat in heat. The audience across the country could see the hysterical movement of the bandages, and they could hear the muffled sound of Mr. Wilson's voice as he tried to save the show.

MR. WILSON:

(Bandages fluttering, and the voice coming in weak, but audible.) "I happen to know that you were a demolition expert during World War II."

DETECTIVE:

"As for you, Mr. Wilson, I happen to know that you were a demolition expert during World War II!"

(A long pause)

MR. WILSON:

"Go on, go on! . . . No! don't say that! . . ." (The bandages across his mouth started to jump up and

down with abandon.) "I also happen to know that
Tony was in your outfit! . . . Isn't that true, Mr.
Wilson? . . . Nod your head if you admit it. . . . I
know you can't talk with all those bandages."

DETECTIVE:

"I also happen to know that Tony was in your outfit . . . isn't that true, Mr. Wilson? . . . Nod your
head if you admit it. . . . I know that you can't talk
with all those bandages." (This was the funniest line
in the whole incident, because several million people
could hear Mr. Wilson talking through the bandages
as he prompted the detective.)

MR. WILSON:

(Bandages fluttering) "Turn to Tony. . . . Don't say
it . . . just turn to Tony. . . . Now, say this: 'Tony!
You were also a demolition expert, in the same outfit as Mr. Wilson . . . *but* you did not construct the
bomb that you *thought* you placed in Mrs. Wilson's
car!'"

DETECTIVE:

(Turning to Tony) "Tony, you were also a demolition expert, in the same outfit as Mr. Wilson . . . *but* you did not construct the bomb that
you *thought* you placed in Mrs. Wilson's car!"

This hilarious nightmare continued for another ten seconds. Then the detective regained his memory and went on to
finish the scene in fine style. It could only have happened during the days of live television. . . . You'll never see anything
like it again.

During the years at CBS, and the five years of free-lance directing, I only directed one sports event. It happened early in my directing career, and after I tell you about that tragic afternoon, you'll know why I never got a chance to direct *another* sports event.

One terrible Saturday morning in 1954, I received a frantic phone call from the boss of the CBS sports department.

"Hello, is this Ken Whelan? . . . Do I know you? . . . Look, I've got a big problem. . . . Have you ever directed a horse race?"

"Yes, this is Ken Whelan . . . And, I don't know if you know *me*, because I don't know who *you* are. . . . No, I've never directed a horse race."

He identified himself, and then he told me all about his big problem. "Look, we're supposed to cover the feature race at Pimlico this afternoon, right?"

"Well, you should know. You're the head of the sports department."

"Don't be a wiseass! Are you *sure* I don't know you? I know a lot of wiseasses! . . . Look, like I said, we're supposed to televise the feature race at Pimlico this afternoon, right? . . . The tech guys are already down there, and they're setting up the cameras right now. . . . There's only one thing wrong. I don't have a director!"

"I have never directed a horse race, sir. . . . With all due respect, I think you've got the wrong director . . . *and* you're absolutely right, I *am* a wiseass."

"I don't care if you're a wiseass! I'm in trouble. . . . My regular director had his appendix removed two hours ago, and I have this crazy idea that he's not going to show up at Pimlico! . . . I need a director!"

"But, why me, sir? . . . I have never directed a horse race, sir. In fact, I have a lot of trouble directing *people*. . . . Did someone recommend me?"

"*Nobody* recommended you! . . . Lou gave me the names of four staff directors who had the day off. . . . You were the only one who answered the phone."

"Oh."

"Now, get your wiseass down to La Guardia airport, catch the first plane to Baltimore, take a cab out to Pimlico, and be there by one o'clock this afternoon! . . . Or else you're going to get your wiseass fired out of CBS!"

"I understand."

I arrived at Pimlico racetrack fifteen minutes before one o'clock. I could have arrived sooner, but the fear of losing my job did not overcome the fear of trying to direct the feature race at Pimlico. On the plane coming down to Baltimore, I had moments when I wished that the plane would crash, I would miss the horse race, and I would end up in the hospital with a couple of broken legs. I figured that a couple of broken legs would be less painful than what I would go through that afternoon. . . . And I was right.

I had to buy a ticket to get into the racetrack, so help me God. They wouldn't let me in until I bought a ticket. I had my CBS identification card on me, and my Directors' Guild card, but they told me I couldn't get in unless I had a special red tag pinned on my coat.

Once inside the racetrack, I couldn't find the CBS truck. The truck was the center of operations for any "remote job" that happened outside a television studio. I spent fifteen minutes looking for the truck, feeling as lost and lonely as on the first day I went to kindergarten. I finally discovered a camera cable running down some stairs, so I followed the cable to the truck.

The technicians gave me the sort of welcome that a rabbi would get in Cairo. They knew nothing about the regular director's appendix trouble, and they were *not* happy to see me.

"Yeh, he had his appendix taken out this morning, so they

sent me down to direct this thing. . . . So, I'd appreciate any help you guys can give me. . . . I've never directed a horse race before."

"That's great," said the technical director. "It's going to be one of *those* afternoons."

The fact that the crew greeted me with cold disdain had nothing to do with me personally. It had to do with the crew it- self. This particular group of technicians were specialists at televising sports events, and they were a tightly knit gang who had been together a long time. They were called "The Dead End Kids" for several obvious reasons. Most of the guys were unmarried rascals who did not like the discipline of working in the New York studios. They preferred the freedom of traveling around the country doing these sports remotes. Some of them were woman chasers, or heavy drinkers, who enjoyed living in motels, and there were a few of them that really enjoyed doing sports events. When you put them all together, they were "The Dead End Kids" who treated *everyone* with cold disdain.

With great reluctance, they took me on a short tour of the racetrack, pointing out the various camera positions. When I asked for a rundown of the things I was supposed to shoot, the technical director was very patient with me. At least, he *thought* he was being very patient with me.

"Look, don't worry about it. . . . *We* know what we're doing. . . . We do it every week. . . . Look, don't worry about it!"

"Right! I understand. . . . I *know* you guys have it under control. . . . You've been doing it for years, and I have abso- lute faith in you. . . . But could you just give me a *hint* of what we're supposed to do? . . . It would make me feel more like a director."

The technical director gave me a scornful look. "OK, if that's the way you want to play it, I'll go along with you. I recognize the symptoms. . . . You really want to direct this thing, don't you?"

"Well, sure . . . that's what they sent me down here for."

"How the hell can you direct something you've never seen before?"

"That's why I want you to run the thing down for me! . . . C'mon, be a good guy."

"I said I would, didn't I? . . . But I'll tell you something right now! . . . No matter how much I fill you in, you *not* going to direct this horse race! . . . Wait and see, it happens fast . . . you won't know what's going on."

"Cut it out. . . . Run it down for me."

The technical director sighed, and led me to the racetrack club house. I had to prime him with two whiskey sours, but he kept his word. With the attitude of a father explaining sex to a twelve-year-old son, he told me what was supposed to happen.

"We open with a wide shot of the racetrack on camera four. . . . That's the camera up on the roof of the grand-stand. . . . Charlie, the audio guy, hits the quarter-inch tape, and the music comes up. . . . We take camera two on Sammy in the paddock. . . . Sammy runs down the horses in the race, tells us about the jockeys, and then he does a three-minute in-terview with the governor of Maryland. . . . Then . . ."

"Who's Sammy?"

"Aw, f'Christ's sake!" he ordered a double whiskey sour. "Sammy's the master of ceremonies . . . the television host for the race. . . . Sammy Resnick, the ex-jockey. . . . He's famous, f'Christ's sake!"

"Oh, sure. . . . I should have known. I'm not much of a racetrack fan."

The technical director was disgusted with me, but he kept his word, and finished his list of things I should know. I sat there like an idiot, writing everything down.

When we got on the air, I found out that the technical director had been telling me the truth. It happened fast, very fast. All of my detailed notations were useless. I just sat there in the truck, watching the monitors and feeling like a visitor. The whole thing happened automatically. The cameramen got their shots without a word of direction. The technical director put the shots on the air with calm purpose. They were a well-oiled machine doing a job they knew how to do.

Then, it happened. . . .

The horses came out of the final turn, and started to pound their way down the home stretch toward the finish line. It was a six-horse race with the three leading horses bunched together up in front. The other three horses were bunched together about twenty yards behind the first group. Camera one had a nice wide shot covering all of the horses in the race.

This was the moment I picked to exercise my directorial powers. I happened to glance at camera three's monitor, and noticed that he had a tight shot of the three leading horses. Being a creative director, I decided that the tighter shot of the three horses was more exciting than the wide shot on camera one.

"Take three," I said, in my firm director-type voice.

The technical director took a quick look at camera three's monitor. "Naw, you don't want me to take three."

"Yes, I do! It's a nice tight shot of the three leaders. C'mon, hurry up! Take three!"

"Naw. We always use the wide shot for the finish."

"Goddammit! I haven't done a thing all day! Now take three! That's an order!"

"All right! All right!" He punched down on camera three's button with an angry finger, and the tight shot of the three horses appeared on the air monitor. It was an exciting moment. The roar of the crowd grew louder as the horses thundered down the stretch.

Then a strange thing happened. The crowd suddenly became quiet. It was a weird feeling. The crowd just stopped roaring, and the three horses on the air monitor were still thundering down the stretch toward the finish line.

"Oh, my God!" yelled the technical director. "Do you know what we've done?"

My eyes were glued to the air monitor as I watched the three horses cross the finish line in complete silence. I still didn't realize what had happened.

The technical director stared at me. His face was completely drained of blood. "We had the WRONG horses! . . . You and your goddamn tight shot! . . . We carried the *last* three horses across the finish line!"

Then, being a professional, he went back to finishing the show. He punched up the wide shot, showing the horses returning to the winner's circle; he took the necessary shots of Sammy explaining the winning ceremony; and then he took the show off the air.

"What happened?" I asked.

"Nothing much. . . . But we've just had a *first* on network television! . . . The race was *over*, do you understand? . . . It was all over, and we carried the three *losers* across the finish line! . . . Wow! . . . Boy oh boy! . . . Do you realize that millions of viewers are *very* confused right now? . . . According to the shot *we* had on the air, the number six horse won the race! . . . But one minute later we show the number two horse wearing the winner's wreath! . . . It's a first, no doubt about it . . . . It's a first!"

"But how could it happen? . . . Why did camera three have a tight shot of the three losers?"

"The man on camera three has a severe drinking problem . . . he had a terrible childhood . . . and he just caught the clap! . . . What do you expect from a guy like that?"

"But . . ."

"My God! Do you know what we've done?"

"Don't cop out, Ken. . . . C'mon, admit it . . . a good director would have *known* that he had the wrong three horses. . . . Right?"

"I guess so, but I've never directed a horse race before. . . . How would I know that?"

"Exactly right. . . . How would you know? . . . That's exactly what I've been trying to tell you all day! How *could* you know? You've never done it before! . . . I'll admit that when I glanced up at the monitor, *I* didn't realize that he had the wrong horses. . . . But I would never have taken that shot! . . . It was wrong, just wrong."

"Yeh, I guess you're right. I should have kept my mouth shut."

Then we both looked at each other, and burst out laughing. We just sat there and laughed. When I got my breath, I yelled, "So you think we had a first! . . . Never been done before! . . . Are you sure?"

"No doubt about it, we had a first! . . . We've just made history! . . . Now, let's go up to the club house and see how many whiskey sours we can drink. . . . One of us is going to be fired, so we might as well go out in style."

As we were leaving the truck, the phone started to ring. The technical director picked it up, listened a moment, and then handed it to me. "It's for you. . . . It's the boss."

I took the phone and put it to my ear. The voice on the other end was very angry:

"Is this Mr. Whelan?"

"Yes . . ."

"Is this the Mr. Whelan I sent down to Pimlico to direct the feature race?"

"Yes, but. . . Look, let me explain. . . . Did it look bad? . . . I mean, do you think anyone noticed the mistake?"

"You're kidding! . . . At this moment, you have been off the air for exactly four minutes. During that four minutes we have received several hundred phone calls from screaming sports fans. . . . The switchboards look like the Fourth of July!"

"They noticed, uh?"

"Tell me something. . . . How did you manage it? . . . Carrying the wrong three horses across the finish line isn't easy to do! . . . I've never seen anything like that in my life!"

"Look, I made a mistake. . . . I admit it. . . . Everyone makes a mistake once in a while. . . . After all, I'm only human."

"No, you're not! . . . You're not human! . . . You know what you are? . . . You're exactly what I called you this morning! . . . You're a wiseass!"

He hung up.

I did not get fired. Fortunately, the voice on the telephone was a nice guy. He got together with the technical director, and between the two of them, they cooked up a phony story that saved my ass. . . . I mean, they saved my wiseass.

One of the craziest incidents I can remember had to do with a horse. It happened on a one-shot special for kids, based on the old *Beauty and the Beast* story. The horse was an important part of the play, so we hired one of the best animal trainers in the business to supply us with an equestrian actor.

The horse and his trainer arrived exactly on time, and the horse zipped through rehearsals like an old pro. In fact, the horse looked disgusted when one of the actors blew his lines.

I was the assistant director on the show, and, as the clock ticked down to air time, I knew that a lot of people connected with the show were worried about a lot of things. But none of us were worried about the horse. He seemed to be the most dependable thing on the show. You'll notice I referred to the horse as *he* . . . that's very important. It may not seem important that the horse was a stallion, but if he had been a mare, this story would never have happened. About halfway through the air show, before the horse was supposed to make his entrance, everything was going well, so we all started to relax a little bit. Then the nightmare started. The stage manager came running into the control room, his face showing white through a deep tan. His eyes looked like Peter Lorre's eyes, and there were flecks of foam at the corners of his mouth.

The moment he burst into the control room, we all knew that we were in deep trouble. Stage managers were not supposed to run into control rooms during an air show. They were supposed to stay backstage. That's why they were called stage managers. Up until that moment, I had never *seen* a stage manager in a control room during an air show. Especially one who looked as if he were having a nervous breakdown.

The director took command, and said, "What are you doing in here, Harry? . . . Is something wrong?"

"It's the horse!"

"The horse? . . . What about the horse?" asked the director.

"He has an erection," answered the stage manager.

"A what?" asked the director.

"A hard-on, sir! . . . The horse has a . . ."

"I heard you. . . . I heard you!" said the director.

The stage manager was almost hysterical. "You should see it! It's unbelievable!"

"That's enough! I don't need a graphic description!" cried the director. "That crazy animal trainer must have brought us a stallion!"

"Something like that," I said. "It's the only kind of horse that can have an erection."

"OK, Mr. Whelan! Since you think this is a funny situation, *you* handle it! . . . When this commercial is over, I'm going to be busy directing this show! . . . I don't want to hear any more nonsense about horses who are sexually excited! . . . In eight minutes I want an impotent stallion to walk on that stage! . . . Solve it, Mr. Whelan!"

By now, the stage manager had lost control, and was blubbering. "We *can't* put that horse on camera! . . . It's the craziest thing you've ever seen! . . . I mean, there might be some children watching! . . . Or Catholics! . . . People like that!"

I hustled the stage manager out of the control room.

"Look, calm down!" I said. "You've got eight whole minutes to solve this problem. . . . What about a cold shower? . . . They say cold showers work real good."

"A cold shower? . . . Are you nuts? . . . Where the hell can I give a twelve-hundred-pound horse a cold shower?"

"You're right. . . . Wait a minute! . . . I've got it! . . . Ice cubes! . . . That's the answer . . . ice cubes!"

"Ice cubes?"

"Ice cubes! . . . The stagehands have a refrigerator in the prop room. . . . Empty the ice trays, and rub the horse with the ice cubes."

"Rub the horse *where* with the ice cubes?"

"Where the hell do you *think* you'd rub the ice cubes? . . . You've got seven minutes."

"*Me*, rub . . . Are you crazy? . . . I'm a happily married man! . . . I couldn't do a thing like . . ."

"You've got less than seven minutes, *and* your career in television may be at stake! . . . Get the ice cubes!"

The stage manager made some strange noises deep down in his throat, and then ran through the door that led to the backstage area. The last words I heard him say were, "Oh, my God! If my mother ever finds out about this!"

In the control room, we practically held our breath for the

next six minutes. We did our jobs, but we didn't talk to each other, because in the back of our minds was a mental picture of a passionate stallion walking into several million living rooms.

Finally, the horse was cued to walk on stage. Camera two had a wide shot to cover the horse's entrance. Camera three was on the air with a single shot of the actor who cued the horse to come in. The director's eyes were glued to camera two's monitor, as drops of sweat gathered on his forehead. He had an important decision to make. If the horse walked into camera two's wide shot displaying his virility, the director *could not* put that shot on the air, and the show would be a disaster. If the horse looked respectable, he could take the shot, and the show would continue in fine style.

The horse walked on stage looking proper enough to take to church. There wasn't a hint of his former condition. For one awful moment, I had the feeling that the ice cubes hadn't worked, and that the stage manager had turned the stallion into a eunuch.

When the show was over, the director turned to me and said, "Congratulations, Whelan. . . . I don't know what you told that stage manager, but it worked."

"Ice cubes," I said.

"Ice cubes?"

"Forget it."

Later on, I congratulated the stage manager. "You did a helluva job. . . . I really didn't think you had the guts to do the ice cube bit."

"I didn't have the guts. . . . I found a seventy-five-year-old stagehand who didn't care *what* he rubbed with ice cubes."

CHAPTER 11

Coward
and
Hayes

There is an old bromide in show business that goes something like this: "The bigger the star, the nicer they are." The inference is that the really big stars have reached a plateau of success, and can afford to be "nice folks." This myth is based on dubious logic. Show people tend to be childlike, and they love to invent fairy tales about their profession. They believe that performers struggling to get to the top are vicious clawing animals who will stop at nothing to achieve success. But the moment these wild animals achieve stardom, according to the myth, they turn into pussy cats. Show people believe that stardom is security, and once secure, a performer can afford to be gracious. Crazy, right? But I've heard this nonsense for years.

I have worked with "stars" in Broadway musicals who would make Jack the Ripper look like a social worker. I have worked with "stars" in television who wouldn't give their mother an autograph. No, the fairy tale doesn't hold true. But I have a variation of this myth that I really believe in. I'll tell you about it later, after I tell you about two "stars" who were pussy cats, nice folks, and very gracious.

A couple of months after I had been promoted to a full-fledged director, I was assigned to direct a one-minute "promo" featuring Helen Hayes, the first lady of the American theater.

A "promo" is a one-minute bit on television that promotes an upcoming network show. You see them all the time. They fit them into station breaks and commercial breaks, and they usually feature the star of the show that they're promoting. If Bob Hope is doing one of his specials some Sunday night, you can count on Bob popping into your living room at least thirty times prior to the show, informing you that if you miss his big special, you should tell it to a priest the next time you go to confession.

Now remember, this promo was only one minute long. I mean, I could hold my breath while I was directing it, and after it was over, I could have made it to the nearest bar before I exhaled. But the name "Helen Hayes" turned me into rice pudding. During the three days leading up to this one-minute epic, I stopped being my usual neurotic self and became a psychopath. I went from manic to depressive, and back again to manic, every five minutes.

During the manic daydreams, I created little scenarios in which my masterful directing techniques prevented this grand lady of the theater from making a fool of herself. These dreams of glory usually ended up with a dialogue that went something like this:

H. HAYES:

"Thank God they assigned *you* to direct this promo, Ken. . . . May I call you Ken?"

ME:

"Please do, Helen. . . ."

H. HAYES:

"Of course, you realize what you've done. . . . This one-minute promo, with your directing genius, has given me a new faith in my acting career."

ME:

"Your talent has always been there, Helen. . . . All I did was release it."

H. HAYES:

"With you directing me, Ken, I could show the world what acting is all about."

ME:

"You are the violin, Helen . . . the instrument. I am simply the artist who plucks your strings, and brings forth the beautiful music."

H. HAYES:

"Promise me that you will always be my director! Promise me that you will direct all of my Broadway plays, and my motion pictures. . . . Just promise me, I won't ask you to sign anything!"

ME:

"I'll think about it, Helen. . . . I'll think about it."
Etc., etc., etc.

PICTURE NUMBER 1

THE SCENE:

A television studio Helen Hayes is lying on the floor of the studio, sobbing hysterically, and pointing an accusing finger at *me.* I try to apologize for my clumsy directing, but she will hear none of it. Finally, she tears up my Directors' Guild membership card, and storms out of the studio.

PICTURE NUMBER 2

THE SCENE:

The lobby of the CBS building I emerge from the elevator with Frank Stanton, William Paley, and the president of the Directors' Guild. Standing in the lobby is Helen Hayes. She is standing beside a basket filled with rocks. They all stone me for several minutes, until I am finally driven from the building.

PICTURE NUMBER 3

THE SCENE:

A street in Forest Hills, N.Y. It is winter, and it is snowing. I am trudging down the street, carrying a sample copy of *World Book* under my arm. I am trying to sell encyclopedias to Jewish housewives.

THE END

When the day of the promo finally arrived, I was very nervous. The script was exactly one typewritten page in length, and I had studied it so many times that the words didn't make sense to me anymore. I forget the name of the show that Helen Hayes was going to do on television, but it's not important. I *do* remember that CBS built a complete kitchen set to do this one-minute promo.

According to the script, Helen Hayes was supposed to come in a door, walk over to the stove, check something she had in the oven, walk to the kitchen table, sit down and do the promo.

Being an idiot at the time, I had made my directorial decisions as to *how* she was to do these things. I had decided that the firm, masterful approach was right. I wanted to impress Helen Hayes with the fact that I wasn't just another "control room" television director. I wanted to show her that I understood acting problems, and I hoped that she would consider me a creative director. I know it all sounds silly and a little insane, but how many two-month-old television directors get a chance to direct Helen Hayes . . . even for a minute?

Helen Hayes came into the studio fifteen minutes early. I introduced myself, and we had a preliminary talk about the timing of the promo, the location of the make-up room, and whether she wanted coffee or tea with her lunch. I remember that I was neither firm nor masterful during this conversation. I talked too much, and suddenly developed a nervous cough. When the time came for me to order lunch, I didn't know the telephone number of our neighborhood delicatessen.

When we actually started to work on the promo, I made my suggestions in the form of an apology. She listened, and did exactly as I said. We shot two takes on camera, and I realized that something was wrong. It didn't look right, it didn't sound right, it was just plain terrible.

I called a five-minute break for the technical crew, and had a short meeting with Helen Hayes. By now, the masterful approach had oozed out of me with my sweat. I was approaching panic. I made a couple of hysterical suggestions, retired to the control room, and shot another take. . . . It was still terrible. I walked out into the studio with visions of Forest Hills, Jewish housewives, and encyclopedias going through my head.

Then Helen Hayes did a wonderful thing. She said something to me in a very loud voice, so that everyone in the studio could hear it.

> This is what she said: "Ken, you're being very patient with me, and I appreciate it. . . . I think your ideas are great, but I just can't seem to do it the right way. . . . I'm an old war-horse who is very set in her ways. . . . I have my bag of tricks, and I guess I'm too old to learn any new tricks. . . . Would you indulge an old lady, and let me try it my way?"

We tried it her way, and of course it was wonderful and exactly right. When she was leaving the studio, she came over to me, and said (again in a loud voice), "You're a charming and talented director. Thank you for being so kind."

Could the queen of England do any better? How often in your lifetime do you meet a human being with such graciousness, tact, and just plain "class"? Obviously, she had come to the conclusion that my directorial choices were wrong. But she kept it to herself. Instead of blaming *me* for the three bad takes, she blamed herself. And she did it in front of the technical crew, the stagehands, and everyone else who was in the studio. She wanted to make sure that I didn't lose face in front of the people I worked with every day. Fantastic, right?

Helen Hayes has been called the grand lady of the theater for many years. The term "grand lady" is usually based on her acting ability, her talent for playing a wide variety of parts,

"Could the queen of England do it any better?"

and the fact that she has been a cornerstone of the American theater for more than fifty years. Believe me, she is a much greater lady *off-stage*. I know, because she saved my rear end one day in the early fifties.

Following the Helen Hayes episode, I was happy to go back to directing cooking shows, morning talk shows, and roller skating derbies. I was smart enough to realize that I was not ready to direct people like Helen Hayes, even if it was for only a minute.

One month later, I was assigned to direct four promos with Noel Coward, and I didn't understand why they picked me again. My feelings about the Helen Hayes promo were guilty feelings. I knew that I had goofed it, and had been rescued by a gracious lady. Two days after being assigned to do the Noel Coward promos, I discovered that I had underestimated the lady's graciousness. I found out that she had said nice things about me to a certain CBS executive. At the time, it was like the kiss of death. I was smart enough to realize that I was not ready to direct people like Noel Coward, even if it was for only four minutes.

This time around, there were no manic daydreams. No visions of being a hero, and zooming to fame. I had the cold sweats for ten days prior to the shooting date.

When the day finally arrived, I walked into the studio and found eleven CBS executives waiting to greet me. They had "dropped in" to give me a little briefing on how to handle Noel Coward. They told me that Mr. Coward had been giving them a lot of trouble during the past week. They told me that Mr. Coward was a difficult man to work with. They described him with words like "temperamental," "emotional," and "stubborn." They were very nervous about Mr. Coward, and by the time they got through their briefing, I was petrified.

I retreated to a chair in the back of the studio and waited for my executioner. I tried to remember the instructions I had received from the executives: "Treat him with kid gloves." "For God's sake, don't argue with him!" "If he wants to do the promos standing on his head, let him!" . . . Etc., etc.

Noel Coward arrived exactly on time. The eleven executives immediately engulfed him, like the tentacles of an octopus. For the next five minutes they conducted a group ass-kissing session. One exec fell in love with Noel Coward's tie, and told the gang that his life would be a failure if he couldn't possess a tie exactly like Noel's. Another exec expressed his devotion to Mr. Coward's playwriting talent, and to illustrate his devotion, he praised a play that had been written by Philip Barry. Yet another exec wanted to know how Mr. Coward managed to stay slim and trim. The way he asked the question was a high point in the history of embarrassing moments. He said, "I just don't understand how a man of your age can keep himself in such excellent shape. My God, I remember seeing you in the movies when I was a ten-year-old kid, and right now I'm twenty pounds overweight." He really believed that he was doing one helluva job of ass-kissing.

Mr. Coward was obviously annoyed with the whole scene, and broke away by asking a question in a loud voice. "Is there a director assigned to this thing?"

I raised my hand like I used to do in school when I wanted to go to the bathroom. "Right here. . . . I'm the director . . . sir."

I stumbled to my feet as he walked toward me. He shook hands with me, and asked me what my name was.

"Ken . . . uh, Whelan. Ken Whelan, that's my name."

"Good, let's get to work, Ken. I'd like to get out of here in an hour. Which one of these things would you like to do first?"

I told him, he agreed, and we went to work. When I asked

"One executive fell in love with Mr. Coward's tie."

him if he wanted to rehearse with the cue cards before we put it on camera, he told me that he didn't need the cue cards because he had memorized the scripts for the four promos. (Cue cards, also known as idiot cards, were sometimes used instead of the Teleprompter. The script was printed on the cards with black crayon, and the cards were held close to the camera.)

When he told me that he had memorized the promos, I prepared myself for the worst. I had been the associate director for countless promos, and every time a performer claimed that he had memorized the script, it had turned out to be a long, horrible day.

After dismissing the man with the cue cards, Mr. Coward asked me, "How do you want me to do these things? . . . Sitting down . . . standing up . . . how?"

"Well, I've got a high stool up there against the back curtain. I thought that maybe we could start with you sitting on the stool with your back to the camera. Then, on cue, you get up, walk down to the camera, and do the promo. It's simple, and I think it fits you."

He thought the idea was fine, so I asked him if he would like to rehearse it a couple of times.

He didn't think a rehearsal was necessary.

I fingered the roll of Tums in my pocket.

"What kind of time cues do you want, Mr. Coward? . . . We usually give a thirty-second cue, and a countdown from ten seconds."

He told me that wouldn't be necessary. He asked me to set one of the portable studio clocks next to the camera, and forget about the timing, he would do it himself.

It took me about thirty seconds to walk from the studio floor to the control room. In that time, I consumed three of my Tums, and was looking for someone to run out and buy me a gallon of Alka-Seltzer. All of the clues pointed toward a disaster.

Mr. Coward sat on the stool, I rolled the kinescope film, and we were off to the races.

Mr. Coward got off the stool when I cued him, walked down to the exact right mark in front of the camera, and started his promo. Without the cue cards, he did the promo word for word, ending up exactly on time to the second.

I couldn't believe it. It was perfect. There was no need to do a second take.

We finished the four promos in thirty-five minutes, which was a new world record for shooting four promos. I was still sitting in the director's chair, stunned with disbelief, when Noel Coward came into the control room.

"Thanks, Ken. . . . Nice job. . . . Hope we work together again." And then he was gone.

Later on, out in the studio, I was congratulated for doing a superb job of "handling" the difficult Mr. Coward. One of the executives asked me my name, and made a note of it on the back of a business card. He hinted that this day might be the beginning of a great career at CBS. He must have forgotten about me, or lost the business card, because three days later I goofed something, and I was a bum again.

Of course, the whole thing was ridiculous. The fact that the promos were done so quickly, and without problems, had very little to do with me. It had to do with Mr. Coward's being a complete "pro," and an extremely talented man. He came in to do a job, he did it with great skill, and then he went home.

Because of my tremendous *success* with the Helen Hayes and Noel Coward promos, I became the Promo King of CBS. In fact, that's about all I directed for the next six months. I must have done about fifty promos during that time period, and not one of them was as easy to do, or as pleasant to do, as the two I did with these giants of show business.

I discovered that the most "difficult" and "temperamental" people to direct were the hosts of game shows and panel shows. Running a close second for hysterical behavior were shapely sex symbols from Hollywood who had condescended to do a live television show. Some of the best profanity I use today was learned from these dubious ladies.

And that brings me back to the old bromide in show business that goes something like this: "The bigger the star, the nicer they are." It's almost correct, but not quite. It should read, "The more *talented* they are, the nicer they are."

CHAPTER 12

The Down-the-Rabbit-Hole Boys with the Well-Capped Teeth

The Royal Families of most large corporations are usually intelligent people. They own most of the stock of the corporation, which they acquired either by inventing the product they sell or by improving a product they inherited. It takes intelligence to do either of these two things. Sometimes the Royal Family hires a Prime Minister to advise them and watch over the kingdom while the Royal Family is away, and although the Prime Minister might not have Royal Family blood lines, he must have a very superior intelligence. I mean, the Prime Minister can't be some idiot who hangs around making dumb remarks. Not when the Royal Family cuts you in with a bunch of stock

137

and talks a lot about blood lines.

Now, at the other extreme of the ladder you can find a certain amount of intelligence. A few of the peasants *have* to know what they're doing or the business would fall apart. In the TV business, some of the electronic wizards who design, build, and maintain the complicated equipment used in television are actually geniuses. During the early years, I ran into a great many peasants who were intelligent and talented. These laborers were directors, technical directors, cameramen, scenic designers, a few writers, and a couple of producers. Then, of course, there were the serfs who performed in front of the cameras: the actors, comedians, and "personalities" who put their jobs and reputations up for grabs every time they went on the air. Most of these people possessed a certain amount of talent, and some of them were extremely intelligent.

So there you have it. The two plateaus in a television network where you might run into some intelligent minds: the Royal Court at the top of the hierarchy, and the peasants at the bottom. (Remember, during these early days, the networks were *producing their own shows*. These days the networks buy their shows from independent packagers, which takes them out of show business, and gives them an innocent third-party cop out in case the show is a stinker.)

It is obvious that these two levels of intelligence could never meet. I mean, you couldn't have electronic technicians, actors, cameramen, and people of that ilk just dropping into the Royal Court whenever they had a bright idea. I don't care how intelligent these peasants were, it just wouldn't have worked out. It wouldn't work because of a corny cliché . . . "class." Class distinction, and just plain "class."

These Royal Court people are different from us folks. They have a different background, they look different, they change their underwear every two hours (they don't wash it, they throw it away), they speak differently, and they can wear ten-year-old tweed sport jackets to a horse show with complete success. It's just plain "class."

The television business wasn't three days old when the Royal Court realized the problem. They *knew* that they couldn't spend their days dealing with people who wore Thom McAn shoes, lived in the *southern* part of Long Island, and graduated from C.C.N.Y.

The intelligent people in the Royal Court had to find some means of communicating with the intelligent people who existed on the other side of the moat.

They solved the problem by hiring a group that I called "The Down-the-Rabbit-Hole Boys." These fellows were middle executives who formed a third plateau, and served as liaison officers between the other two plateaus.

The basic requirements for being a middle executive were slightly mysterious. After years of observing these creatures, I came to the conclusion that the first requirement had to do with the way they *looked*. It seemed to me that they had to look *something* like the Royal Court people, but not *exactly* like the Royal Court people. The haircuts were the same. (In those days, hair was close cropped so it wouldn't show below their helmets.) Their clothes were *almost* the same as the Royal Court fellows, but not *quite* the same. It had to to with tailors. A Down-the-Rabbit-Hole guy would never dream of discussing tailors with a Royal Court guy, because it might leave the impression that the Rabbit-Hole guy had pretensions far beyond his station.

Another requirement was that they possess a rather hazy and undistinguished background. I found it very difficult to discover what some of these middle executives did for a living *before* they bought the house in Greenwich, Connecticut. I think blood lines had a lot to do with it. Not *Royal* blood lines.

God forbid. But maybe bastard blood lines, where a distant cousin to the Royal Family had married a guy from Boston who wrote the lyrics to a Harvard Hasty Pudding Show in 1921, the union bringing forth a son who was pure White Anglo-Saxon Protestant, but who looked Jewish. This son would have all of the requirements for being a middle executive. Half-assed blood lines, a touch of culture (the Hasty Pudding Show in 1921), and because of his beliefs and looks he could deal with *any* sponsor who wasn't Catholic. (I don't remember too many Catholic sponsors, but if there were a few, I'm sure there was a middle executive who could handle them.)

One of our middle executives, whom I knew for years, was always talking about his theatrical background. He never went into details, but I assumed that he was a former Broadway producer or director who had seen better days (he was elderly). This assumption led me to treat him with a certain amount of respect, in spite of the fact that he never said anything that could be interpreted. I found out later that his only experience in the theater was a play he had backed in 1934. The play received the worst reviews of the season, and he had lost forty thousand dollars. In retaliation, he never set foot in a theater again, and refused to read the drama page of *any* newspaper. Of course, all of this was the reason he never talked sense. He thought Mary Martin was Ethel Merman, Brando was Paul Brando, because he got Paul Newman and Marlon Brando mixed up, and he was always trying to get in touch with the agent of some actor who had been dead for ten years.

Their talent for not making too much sense was why I named these fellows "The Down-the-Rabbit-Hole Boys with the Well-Capped Teeth." They talked Alice in Wonderland talk. It sounded like they all had the same writer, and his name was Lewis Carroll. Let me give you an example.

Due to an unfortunate chain of events, I became involved

in a show called "Joe and Mabel," starring Larry Blyden and Nita Talbot. (You might remember it if you have a remarkable memory. It *did* get on the air, and it did last a *few* weeks, and if you do remember it, you're a television freak.) Larry Blyden played a cab driver who was courting Nita Talbot, who played a telephone operator, or a secretary, or something like that. Both of them were great, as they always were, and always will be. The basic trouble with the show had nothing to do with the acting, the directing, the writing, etc. The show bombed because the original concept was hopeless. But at the time we were doing it, no one seemed to be aware of this little truth, including me.

Incidentally, I was not the director or producer of this show. I was a spy. That's right, I was a CBS spy.

The show was a David Susskind package, in conjunction with CBS. This means that they were partners. As partners, they were very suspicious of each other, so there were a lot of spies hanging around. My official title was "CBS Liaison Producer," which meant that I was the chief spy. I was supposed to keep an eye on things, report the progress of the show to my superiors, and put the finger on any of Susskind's people who looked like goof balls.

During the first few days of rehearsal, I had absolutely nothing to report. It was the first show of the series, so everyone was kind of feeling their way along, hoping for the best. To tell the truth, I knew less about the show than anyone involved, so I just kept my mouth shut and watched. The director was Dan Petrie, who looked very competent. I thought the cast was great, the scenery was well done, and Susskind had a right-hand man named Bob Costello who impressed me as being a pretty sharp apple. I thought everything was just fine, so I made no reports.

About two days before the show was supposed to go on the

air, I received a phone message from my boss. He wanted a meeting with me right away, and he told me not to show up wearing brown shoes. (He had a thing against brown shoes.)

When I walked into his office, I had the same feelings I always had when I walked into his office. My pants suddenly felt baggy and in need of a pressing. My fingernails became grimy, and I made a mental note to start getting manicures twice a week. I resisted the urge to postpone the meeting until I had taken a quick shower, visited the barber, and bought a gallon of the most expensive men's cologne.

You see, this particular Rabbit-Hole guy featured good grooming. In fact, good grooming was his complete identity. Very few people could remember his name, so they'd refer to him as the guy with the crazy fingernails who smelled so good. If he had been a bachelor, and his salary had been less, they would have called him a faggot.

"Whelan, you haven't made any reports on this 'Joe and Mabel' thing! What seems to be the problem?"

"You've just answered it, sir. . . . I don't think there *are* any problems. I think it's going fine."

"That's not what the other guys say."

"*What* other guys? . . . I thought *I* was the chief spy! I beg your pardon. . . . I mean chief liaison producer."

"Oh, c'mon, Whelan, don't be naive. . . . Incidentally, where do you have your hair styled? You can't go on with hair like that."

"*What* other guys? . . . Are you saying that you have spies who are spying on *me?* . . . That's obscene! . . . Don't you trust me?"

"It has nothing to do with trust, you know that. It's just the way we operate."

"It's the hair, right? . . . These other spies have better haircuts than I have. . . . That's the answer, isn't it?"

"Oh, for God's sake, Whelan! Sometimes I think you have a touch of paranoia! But it wouldn't hurt if you asked around and found a decent barber." He checked his own hair with a silver pocket mirror and sprayed something into his mouth. "This is a big business, Whelan. One man's opinion just isn't enough. The other spies aren't spying on *you*, that's ridiculous. It's just our way of getting a diversity of opinion."

"I'm shocked, sir. . . . I want you to know that I am really shocked. I had no idea this sort of thing was going on."

"Why don't you try Ralph? He's located in the Pierre Hotel."

"Huh?"

"He's a barber. Of course, he's not *my* barber, but some of the lower executives have found him adequate."

"Oh, the hair again. . . . What did you say? Ralph in the Pierre Hotel, right?"

"It would be a step forward, Whelan. It really would."

"But, do you think it would be proper for a lowly director to walk around looking like an executive? Even a minor executive. I mean, wouldn't it be pretentious?"

"Forget it, Whelan. Just keep wearing those suits you wear, and there'll be no problem of identification."

"I understand. . . . Now, let's get back to the spying business. Just what are the other spies saying that I'm not saying?"

"Well, one thing they're saying is that the show isn't too funny."

"That's a lot of bunk. *I* think it's funny."

He started to leaf through a copy of last week's Nielsen ratings, completely ignoring me. He wasn't reading the thing, it was just his version of the Executive Scolding Bit. You see, I had just made a definite statement of a definite opinion which obviously disagreed with his opinion (even though he had never seen *one* of the rehearsals). What he really wanted to say was, "You stupid son-of-a-bitching show business creep! How dare you walk into my office with those white sweat socks, and give a personal opinion about *anything!* Either shape up and play the game, or stay away from me!"

But he was afraid to say all this, because I just might be shooting my mouth off to a lot of people, and he wasn't sure who I knew. If I went around telling people I thought the show was great, and that he thought the show was a bomb, *and* the show turned out to be a hit . . . then he might be in trouble.

He stared at a few more pages of the ratings, putting me in my place, and reminding me that personal opinions in *his* office were taboo.

Finally, he closed the rating book. "So *you* think the show is funny?"

"Yes, I do. . . . I don't know if it will get ratings, but I think it's funny. . . . I don't think the show is in any trouble!"

"Well, you may be right, Whelan. . . . I certainly wouldn't disagree with you. But, we're after a diversity of opinion, and the other guys say that the show could stand a few more jokes."

"Jokes?"

"Personally, I have no opinion at all. . . ." (Here it comes.) . . . "Unfortunately, I've been too busy to drop in on the rehearsals . . ." (Now, listen to this.) . . . "I'm relying on you guys who are *on the scene* to feed me the right information" (There it is. The perfect middle-executive cop-out. He has just absolved himself from any responsibility.)

"I'm feeding you the only information I have, sir. I think it's going great."

"I pray that you're right, Whelan, I really do. However, we must go along with the rule about diversity of opinion. . . . Do you own a hairbrush, Whelan?"

"Huh?"

"How do you comb your hair?"

"With a comb!"

"I thought so!! There's one of your problems, Whelan. Buy yourself a good hairbrush. But, make sure it's a pure bristle, and not one of those cheap nylon brushes. It will cost you a little more money, but it's a good investment in your future."

"Pure bristle, right!"

He picked up a few sheets of paper from his desk and handed them to me. "Here are some jokes I want you to insert in the show. Give them to Susskind and Costello, they'll know what to do with them."

I made the mistake of smiling. "I'm *sure* they'll know what to do with them."

"Look, Whelan, I can do without your Brooklyn satire. Just get these jokes into the show, and cut out the sarcasm."

"But this is crazy! You can't stick a bunch of random jokes into a situation comedy!"

"It's three-to-one against you, Whelan. Diversity of opinion, remember? The *other* liaison guys say that the show needs some laughs."

"That's not what I mean! . . . OK, maybe the show does need a few more laughs, but *this* isn't the answer! The humor in a situation comedy comes from the situations these particular characters get into! If it isn't funny, it's because the characters are wrong and the situations are wrong! . . . You just can't add a lot of jokes and make it work! . . . It's insane!"

He started to read the Neilsen ratings again, and I knew he was annoyed. "You show business people are a pain in the ass. You think you're the only ones who know anything about putting on a show. *I* know all about situations and character and that sort of stuff. . . . My God, do you think I could be an important executive in programming if I didn't understand the basics of situation comedy?"

"Then how can you ask me to stick three pages of assorted jokes into this show? Bob Costello will probably hit me right in the mouth!"

"You must think I'm a complete fool, Whelan. Do you *really* think I would give you three pages of assorted jokes, and expect you to put them into a situation comedy?"

"But, you . . ."

"What is the profession of the male protagonist in the show?"

"He's a cab driver, you know that."

"Of *course* I know that. . . . Now, would you say that the fact he drives a cab has anything to do with his character, or that the situations have anything to do with the fact that he drives a cab?"

"Absolutely! It's fifty percent of the show . . . but . . ."

"Whelan, you underestimate me. The three pages I have given you are not filled with *assorted* jokes. Those pages contain forty-nine of the greatest cab-driving jokes that have ever been written."

"What?"

"Now, go put them in the show and stop the nonsense."

"But . . ."

"Get out of here! You're making me late for lunch."

I backed toward the door, staring at the typewritten pages I held in my hand. As I opened the door, his parting words reached me through a mist of disbelief.

"Don't forget about the hairbrush, Whelan . . . pure bristle!"

(Incidentally, the forty-nine cab driver jokes were never used on the "Joe and Mabel" show. I threw them into a trash basket on Madison Avenue.)

The middle executive ranks did not have a monopoly on "Rabbit-Hole Boys." We had quite a few executive producers who would have felt right at home at the Mad Hatter's tea party.

First, let me explain what a good executive producer is supposed to be, then I'll tell you about a particular executive I knew back in the good old days. The ordinary viewer doesn't pay much attention to the credits at the end of a TV show. If you are the exception to the rule and actually read this list, you will notice that the last three credits are to the director, the producer, and the executive producer.

Most people have a rough idea about the functions of a director. The more sophisticated viewer thinks he understands the producer's role. But very few people have any idea what an executive producer is supposed to do. I think it's the word "executive" that throws them.

Today, an executive producer is usually the independent packager who owns the show. In the Golden Age of Television, the executive producer worked for the network, but the duties were the same. A good network executive was supposed to come up with an idea for a new show and submit it to his superiors, or he would be assigned an idea for a new show by the gods above.

In either case, once the project had been approved by the bosses, he was required to bring forth a hit show with high ratings. His first step would be to choose a producer for the project. (Remember, our hero is an *executive* producer.) The executive producer and the producer of his choice would then pick a staff of writers. After two months of creative meetings, usually held in the executive producer's favorite East Side bar, he was supposed to send the writers to Fire Island, where they would write the pilot script.

When the writers returned from Fire Island with the pilot

script, the executive producer and producer would decide that the script was unacceptable, suggest changes, and send the writers back to Fire Island. If the writers made too many trips to Fire Island, the executive producer was supposed to banish them to Fire Island for the rest of their lives. He would then start all over again with a new staff of writers.

After the executive producer decided that the pilot script was acceptable, he picked a director (with the approval of the producer, of course). The next step was to assign a budget for the show. The budget had to be high enough to produce a decent production, yet low enough to win approval from the executive producer's superiors. The show would then be cast with the necessary actors, and rehearsals would begin.

From this moment on, the responsible executive producer played the role of mother superior to the entire production staff. He watched everything that was going on, listened to complaints, smoothed ruffled egos, and made creative decisions that he thought were correct. He guided the show toward its birth. That's what a *good* executive was supposed to do. Of course, it meant that he had to be a talented man. He had to have some experience in the theater or motion pictures. He would have to be a strong man, able to accept the results of his own choices, and not blame everyone else if the show was a flop.

I'm sure that there were a few gentlemen of this caliber hanging around during the good old days, but I never had the pleasure of working with them. The executive producers that I encountered were a different breed. They were a shadowy lot who were always making trips to the "Coast," swapping the names of their tailors, or redecorating their offices. I came to the conclusion that the most difficult thing an executive producer had to do was to justify his trip in from Westport every day. Most of them had had very little show business experience before their entrance into television, and one of them had never *seen* a Broadway play. *All* of these fellows agreed that Raymond Massey was America's greatest actor.

I've probably given you the impression that the executive producers I worked with were completely untalented. This is not true. There was one talent that every executive producer possessed in great quantities. Every one of them was a genius in the art of blaming. Their whole lives were devoted to perfecting this art. They worked day and night developing new techniques in the avoidance of responsibility.

The champion of them all was B.J. Tanner, the inventor of the Memo Method. (That's not his real name. I don't want to hurt anyone, and he may have children who respect him. On the other hand, if he did have children, he would have blamed it on a writer or director, so I guess it's silly for me to be secretive.)

B.J. Tanner's track record as an executive producer was nine shows, nine failures. Over a period of three years at CBS, not one of his shows had ever been seen on the air. During these three years his salary was raised each and every year. Illogical? Don't be silly, that's nothing. Before CBS lured him into their camp, B.J. was an executive producer for one of the biggest advertising agencies on Madison Avenue. He worked at the agency for two years. His track record at the agency was six tries, six bombs . . . No successes. Impossible? Fiction? Not at all. Right at this moment, in 1973, B.J. is the executive producer of a popular situation comedy originating in Hollywood. He got the job long after the show had established itself as a winner. The original executive producer (one of the capable ones) was shot by his wife. B.J. became executive producer because of his reputation among network executives as a man who had *never been blamed for a failure!*

The key word is "blame."

B.J. was an expert at the "blame game." He was the inventor of the Memo Method. The way it worked was simple, as all great things are simple. When B.J. was assigned to a show, he would wait until the second week of creative sessions with the writers, then he would send a memo to the vice president in charge of programming.

> To S.G.:
> . . . Pertaining to our future winner, "The Merry Monihans." I grow more convinced every day that *your* basic idea is a dynamite concept for a hit show. I am a little concerned about the ability of the writing staff to live up to the high level of *your* original concept. (I hired the four top writers in the business.) However, I'm sure that I can pull them together and deliver a show worthy of your standards.
>
> Signed,
> B.J. Tanner

The day after the actors had been signed to contracts, the following memo would be sent to B.J.'s boss:

> To S.G.:
> . . . Pertaining to "The Merry Monihans" pilot. Everything going according to schedule. Casting was completed yesterday, with the signing of a talented group of performers. I am a trifle concerned about a few of the producer's choices, but he has a good track record, which justifies my backing him up. A good captain must have faith in his first lieutenant . . .
> It looks like a big one, S.G.
>
> Signed,
> B.J. Tanner

After the show had been in rehearsal for a few days, the memo would read something like this:

> To S.G.:
> . . . A short progress report concerning our rating winner for next season, "The Merry Monihans." I'm very optimistic about the way it's taking shape. Your basic idea of a family that has no visible means of support, and yet seems to be happy without material things, is proving to be a great comedy springboard. The fact that you admit being influenced by William Saroyan only proves your integrity and high level of taste. I'm slightly concerned about our choice of director. The producer and myself were greatly impressed by the fact that he has directed three hit comedy shows in a row. However, my concern is that the particular level of comedy required for our project may not be his kettle of fish. I am trying to guide him toward a more subtle approach, and am convinced that I can pull it off.
>
> Signed,
> B.J. Tanner

B.J.'s memos covered everything that could possibly be blamed on him. The writers, producer, director, scenery designer, lighting director, etc. . . .

If the show was a hit, B.J. was the genius who had whipped the whole thing into shape. If the show was a failure, our hero had a cop-out for everything. He covered himself by telling why he *hired* the staff, then he covered himself by suspecting their talents and stating that he was trying to pull it together. There's no need to go on about this. The greatness of the Memo Method is obvious to anyone who knows anything about the art of blaming.

I was spared a possible shafting by B.J. due to a happy accident. The day after I was assigned to one of B.J.'s pilots, I happened to meet his secretary at an Upper West Side cocktail party. After three shots of Rhine wine she revealed her secret passion for tap dancing. She had studied foot percussion as a child, with the hope of becoming Ann Miller. After six boiler-makers, I exposed myself as an ex-professional tap dancer, and she became my slave for life. A few Rhine wines later, I taught her a complete soft-shoe routine, while she admitted that she hated her boss. I switched her to straight gin and hit the jack-pot . . . She told me about the Memo Method.

The following day, I arrived at B.J.'s office with a note from my doctor. The note excused me from participating in B.J.'s newest project on the grounds that I was suffering from yellow jaundice. My complexion being what it was, B.J. never suspected a thing. He *did* write a memo about it.

CHAPTER 13

The Mystery of "The Red Buttons Show"

"Ho ho, hee hee, ha ha, ho ho. . . . Strange things are happening." Do these words mean anything to you? They were the lyrics of a little song that Red Buttons did on every one of his live TV shows. Remember? He used to cup one hand over his ear as if he were listening to the sound of the ocean in a seashell, and then hop on one foot and then the other foot, like an Indian ceremonial dance.

I can't remember any other lyrics to this little ditty, and I don't think there *were* any more words to the song. He'd just hop around the stage repeating this crazy lyric over and over again. When I watched him do it every week I thought the

153

whole thing was silly, yet the studio audience would break into applause every time Red started this weird ritual. Now, twenty years later, I believe that the "Ho ho, hee hee" song is the main clue to the mystery of "The Red Buttons Show."

But before I do my detective work, I'd like to tell you about the most embarrassing incident that happened to me while I was an associate director. The incident made me the laughing stock of my fellow workers for six months, and was the basis of my undying hatred for all audio technicians.

The traumatic event happened during one of Red's funniest sketches, which took place in an apartment with a lot of doors. I don't remember what the plot was, but I remember that most of the comedy had to do with the doors. The apartment setting had three bedroom doors, a kitchen door, a front door and a back door, a dining-room door, and a bathroom door. The climax of the sketch was a furious chase scene in which two gangsters chased Red Buttons in and out of the various doors in an attempt to shoot him. You've seen this type of scene in Marx Brothers films, Buster Keaton movies, Jack Lemmon movies, and in a couple of Shakespeare's plays. It's an old comedy device that goes back to the Greeks, and for some odd reason it's always funny.

Before I tell you about this crazy thing that happened to me, I have to explain an audio technical term called "cross talk." Cross talk is a mixup in audio connections which enables the home viewer to hear the director's voice, the associate director's voice, or the technical director's voice. It's not supposed to happen; it's a mistake. It still happens once in a while, but because everything is done on tape, the mistake never reaches the home audience. If you have a very good memory, I'm sure you can remember examples of "cross talk" on some of the live shows during the early days of television.

It might have been a mystery show like "Suspense," and while the innocent suspect embraced his loved one, you heard a

"Ho ho, hee hee . . . Strange things are happening." (And they did.)

strange voice saying strange things like, "C'mon, Jack, go in tight! . . . Move that camera right in there! . . . Let's go, I want a *real* tight shot! . . . When they kiss, I want to see their tonsils!" . . . If you heard anything like that, you were hearing the director's voice, and you were also hearing a classic example of "cross talk." With no doubt at all, I'm sure that I was the worst victim of "cross talk" in the history of television, and it happened during this Red Buttons sketch with all the doors.

As I explained earlier in the book, an associate director at CBS "readied" all the camera shots for the director. In other words, he told each camera what the next shot was, and made sure that the shot was correct. During the early part of this particular sketch my "readies" sounded something like this: "Three [camera three] go to bedroom door number two, ready to pull wide. . . . One on the dining room door, a tight shoulder shot of Red . . . no move. . . . Two on the front door wide, to carry Red and the bad guy."

When the tempo of the chase scene became faster, with the gangster and Buttons running in and out of the doors at full speed, my "readies" became shorter and crisper: "Two to the front! . . . Pot shot! No move! . . . Three to the kitchen! Wide! . . . One to the back! To carry!" . . . I didn't have time to say "kitchen *door*," or "back *door*," so I just left out the word "door," and trusted in the talents of the cameramen.

Toward the end of the sketch, the pace became furious, so my instructions were cut to the bare minimum: "Three to kitchen! . . . One to front! . . . Two on bedroom three! . . . One to the dining room!" By this time, things were happening so fast, I didn't even have time to tell the cameramen whether their shot was a tight shot, a medium shot, or a wide shot. I just hoped to God that they remembered the rehearsals, and would come up with the correct lens.

Everything was going great until *it* happened. We were getting to the end of the sketch, "Two to dining room! . . . Three to the bathroom! . . . One to bedroom number two! . . . Three, let's go! . . . The bathroom, the bathroom! . . . Two on the kitchen! . . . C'mon, three what's the matter with you? . . . Go to the bathroom! . . . Go to the bathroom!"

Camera three did *not* get a shot of the bathroom door; instead, the cameraman panned his camera from door to door like a crazy man. "Three, what the hell's the matter?" I yelled. . . . "Go to the bathroom! Go to the bathroom!"

It was at this moment that one of the other cameramen spoke to me on the head set, and told me that camera three couldn't hear a word I was saying and couldn't talk back to me. An audio problem was isolating camera three from the control room, making the cameraman helpless in a sketch as fast as the one we were doing.

We finished the sketch, minus a couple of bathroom door shots, and a few minutes later we were off the air. Everyone in the control room heaved a sigh of relief, happy that we had got through the damn thing without a major disaster. (The missed bathroom shots didn't matter; without a script no one would know the difference.) We were all busy congratulating each other on a fairly smooth show when the telephones began to ring. It wasn't the usual two or three calls that come in after a show goes off the air, it was like every damn phone in the control room was ringing. It sounded like the bells of St. Patrick's Cathedral on Easter morning.

Like a fool, I answered one of the phones. "Yes? . . . 'Red Buttons Show' . . . control room."

An angry voice screamed, "Who am I talking to?"

"Who am *I* talking to? . . . We don't accept anonymous phone calls."

The voice on the phone went up a couple of octaves.

"Anonymous! Anonymous? . . . I happen to be one of the unfortunate sponsors of your goddamn show!"

"I'm sorry you didn't like the show, sir. . . . Personally, I didn't think it was that bad."

"Are you crazy? . . . You have just made my company look ridiculous! . . . You went to my commercial exactly thirty seconds after it happened!"

"I beg your pardon? . . . After *what* happened?"

"What is your name? . . . I demand to know your name!"

My steel-trap mind came up with the guess that something bad had happened, and I didn't want any part of it. "My name? My name is Dave Woo Long. . . . Would you like me to spell that for you?"

The indignant sponsor hung up on me.

At the same time, an angry, hysterical audio man burst out of the audio booth, shouting his head off.

"Oh boy, oh boy! . . . We really did it! . . . We really did it this time! . . . I've been getting phone calls you wouldn't believe!" The audio man headed right for me. "They heard every word you said, Ken! . . . Every son-of-a-bitchin' word! . . . The whole country heard it! . . . Boy oh boy oh boy, are we in trouble!"

I didn't know what the audio man was screaming about. "What is all this *we* crap? . . . I don't remember making any mistakes in the last half hour. . . . What are you talking about?"

"We had cross talk, Ken. . . . Cross talk! . . . Remember when camera three had trouble hearing you? . . . Well, that wasn't the only problem. . . . Every word that camera three *couldn't* hear was heard by the entire network. . . . Oh boy, oh boy!"

I still didn't understand what all the fuss was about. Cross talk had happened on many shows before and it never created this much excitement. The sketch was still a blur in my mind, so I wasn't quite sure *what* I had said to camera three. I looked at the script in front of me, then I leafed back a few of the pages to the tail end of the sketch with the doors. I read a few of camera three's readies, and then I knew the truth. . . . "Three to the bathroom. . . . Go to the bathroom, three! Go to the bathroom! What's the matter with you, three? Go to the bathroom!" . . . Etc.

The technical director handed me a telephone. "For you, Ken. . . . He says that he owns a lot of CBS stock, and that he's on the board of directors."

I took the telephone. "I believe him, Carl, I believe him. . . . I think we've caught the attention of CBS executives who have been underground for years."

"Is this the perpetrator?" asked the voice on the other end of the phone.

"I'm afraid so, sir. . . . At least, it was my voice that you heard."

"Well, I just wanted to tell you that it was the funniest thing I've ever heard on a television show. . . . It was beautiful! . . . Absolutely beautiful!"

"That's very decent of you, sir. . . . I mean, to have that attitude about it. . . . I thought . . ."

"I'm not being decent about it, young man, I'm being a little bit drunk. . . . I'm on my tenth martini and I think the whole thing was beautiful! . . . I may change my mind tomorrow."

"God forbid, sir."

"Well, nice talking to you, young man. . . . It's just possible that you have caused the greatest mass bowel movement since the invention of Ex-Lax."

Now, to get back to the mystery of "The Red Buttons Show." It wasn't a real mystery, of course. I mean it wasn't one of those mysteries where a chorus girl gets poisoned, or anything like that. But, it was a mystery to everyone, and I think I have the solution.

"The Red Buttons Show" was one of the biggest hits in television for a year. And I mean *big*. The show had a rating somewhere in the top ten, but even that fact was no measure of its popularity. During that first season, Red Buttons was a household word, like Coca-Cola or Mickey Mouse. Toward the end of that first season, Red's portrait appeared on the cover of *Time* magazine, which will give you some idea of the popularity of the show.

The show was taken off the air during its second year. The ratings were bad, and, I don't think we made it past Christmass.

The mystery is . . . *what happened?*

It was a first, and it was a last. It had never happened before, and it has never happened since. Oh, there have been lots of shows that were a mild success the first season and bombed out the second year, but in the history of television I don't know of any other show that was a national sensation the first season, yet couldn't make it through the next season.

We did the exact same show the second year that we did the first. The format was the same, the production staff was the same, and if I remember correctly, we had the same technical crew. Red Buttons was the same Red Buttons, the sketches were just as funny, and the coffee was delivered to the studio by the same Joe Vasile, who worked for the same coffee shop.

The mystery is . . . *what happened?*

Now, it's just possible that something happened in the plush offices of the CBS hierarchy that I knew nothing about. I mean, sometimes these shadowy executives make decisions that baffle the mind. But, I don't think so. The fact is, the ratings went down, and the show was taken off the air.

The mystery is . . . why did the ratings go down?

Why did the viewing public make this show a national phenomenon the first year, and destroy it the second year? I remember that a lot of theories were kicked around for a while, but none of them added up to anything, so after a few months we forgot about the theories and chalked it up as one of those things that happen in show business.

Now, twenty years later, I think I have the answer. I got the idea a couple of months ago while I was watching a TV commercial. It was one of those awful pitches for a five-dollar album of nostalgic songs from the "nostalgic fifties." The guy doing the pitch was Red Buttons, so help me God. Before he went into his sales talk, Red did a few seconds of his "Ho ho, hee hee" song, and as I watched this little hunk of nostalgia, the solution to the mystery suddenly occurred to me.

It was the song . . . the ridiculous little song that didn't mean a damn thing . . . "Ho ho . . . hee hee . . . ha ha . . . Strange things are happening." . . . One hand cupped over his ear, and hopping around the stage like a nut. . . . It had no meaning at all, yet it was the answer to why "The Red Buttons Show" was one of the biggest things in the country for one year, and died the next year.

As I watched Red do his pitch for the album, my mind slid back to that first year he was on the air. I remembered my own kids' reaction to the show. Whenever I asked them how they liked the show, they would put one hand over an ear, and hop around the living room, screaming, "Ho ho . . . hee hee," etc. If I went to a party, and Red Buttons' name came up, the reaction was the same. Always the hand over the ear, always the crazy hopping, and of course, "Ho ho . . . hee hee."

Now, I'm not saying that this little song was the only reason for the phenomenal first year. Red did a good show every week, with funny sketches written by the best sketch writers in the business and performed by the best of comedy actors. Looking back, I would say that it was one of the top five comedy shows of the Golden Age, and I think that *without* the "Ho ho, hee hee" song, the show would have had three or four successful years with fairly high ratings. . . . I'm not making sense, right? . . . But, wait a minute, I'm going to explain my theory, and it's this:

For some inexplicable reason, this little song became a ritual to millions of people. Like I said before, the song itself didn't mean a thing. "Ho ho . . . hee hee . . . ha ha . . . Strange things are happening." . . . What the hell does that mean? Does hopping around a stage holding one hand over your ear mean anything? Absolutely not. Yet, it meant *something* to those millions of viewers. I think the cupped hand over the ear meant something like the seashell I mentioned before. I think the audience liked to imagine that Red was hearing things *they* couldn't hear. Maybe it was the sound of the ocean, or perhaps a little piece of wisdom that Red was tuned into. Anyway, I think the whole thing became a ritual because it had all of the ingredients for a successful ritual. It made absolutely no sense at all, not one soul on earth understood what the hell he was doing, yet it hinted at something deep and meaningful. These same ingredients are the basis for the major rituals of the world. The religious, the political, the war rituals, the love rituals, and the dozens of rituals we do every day without really knowing why we do them.

I think that Red's little ritual hinted that the whole world was absolutely crazy, and that the individual television viewer shouldn't worry too much if *he* were slightly crazy. Now, you've got to admit that this was a pretty good little ritual. At least it made a person feel comfortable, which is very rare when it comes to rituals.

Of course, I could be absolutely wrong about why this insane piece of nonsense captured the imagination of so many people. It could have meant different things to different people, but I'm sure about one thing . . . it can take the credit for the fantastic ratings of the first year, and it can be blamed for bombing out the show on the second year.

What happened was very simple. "Ho ho, hee hee" became more important than the show, *or* Red Buttons. A major part of our audience tuned in just to watch this crazy little ritual. Oh, they probably watched and laughed at the rest of the show, but I think that it got to a point where this silly thing *was* "The Red Buttons Show." It became a fad to watch Red cup his hand over his ear, and hop around the stage. It was the thing to do, like wiggling your rear end with a Hula Hoop around your waist, or wearing miniskirts, or swallowing goldfish. It was responsible for the first season's astronomical ratings, and it got Red's portrait on the cover of *Time* magazine. But, like all fads and gimmicks, it faded quickly. The public lost interest in "Ho ho, hee hee," and forgetting that the rest of the show was funny and worthwhile, they tuned to something else the second season.

Well, that's it. That's all there is to it. It's my solution to the mystery of "The Red Buttons Show." I'm sure that Red Buttons himself couldn't care less, but it's one of my pet theories, and I'm glad I said it.

CHAPTER **14**

Instant Images
from the
Golden Age

My memory is a strange, tricky thing. If I'm at a party or just sitting around with friends, and someone mentions a show I directed, my memory coughs up short "one-liner" anecdotes. I seem to forget the frustrations, the phonies, the stomach pains, the second guessers, the failures, etc. I hope that this is the sign of a "healthy" memory, but whatever it is, that's the way it seems to work. I don't know *why* these instant images flash through my mind at the mention of a certain name or a certain show, but they always do, and they're always the same images.

For instance, when a new acquaintance discovers that I once directed "The Big Payoff" for two years, the first thing

165

they want to know is something about Bess Myerson. Now, it just happens that the two quick anecdotes that occur to me about "The Big Payoff" have nothing to do with Bess Myerson, so I'm always at a loss, and these new acquaintances are always disappointed. I have no amusing anecdotes about Bess Myerson, I have no bitchy anecdotes about Bess Myerson, and I have no dirty anecdotes about Bess Myerson. I remember her as an extremely beautiful woman who spoke English fairly well. I admired her because I felt she was working under a tremendous handicap. She had won a Miss America contest, which is the worst stigma that can be placed upon a normal and talented woman. And I was suspicious of her because she had a brain.

Personally, I think Bess was wasting her particular talents on the show, and I'm glad that she finally got out of television and into something where she could use more of her capabilities. On "The Big Payoff" she only had a chance to use her good looks and her regal personality. As Commissioner of Consumer Affairs for New York City, Bess had a chance to use that brain. As a resident of Manhattan, I watched her progress in this very important position, and I thought she did a helluva job. If she ever runs for mayor I'll vote for her twice.

The two quick images that flash into my mind when someone mentions "The Big Payoff" have nothing to do with the show at all. They concern the Brian Houston advertising agency, which was the producing agency for Colgate-Palmolive. In fact, both of these incidents involved the owner of the agency, Mr. Brian Houston, and both took place at that decadent institution, the office Christmas party.

When I signed up to direct "The Big Payoff," the contract was with the Brian Houston agency. I was assigned an office in their building, but during the entire two years I directed the show, I never set foot in it. I did all of my work in the Walt

"She operated under a tremendous handicap."

Framer office over on Sixth Avenue, due to a little tiff with an agency executive the first day I reported for work. Before I could even *find* my office, this executive jumped me and delivered a short lecture on the way I was dressed. He didn't like my brand new sport coat, he didn't like my brand new moccasins (with heels, of course), he didn't like my recently laundered sport shirt, and his nostrils dilated when he discussed my white socks.

I was stunned by the whole thing, because I had made a point of dressing up for my first day at work. I figured that I'd dress formally for my first week, and then after they got to know me, I'd dig out the casual clothes.

Needless to say, I was angry and hurt by this episode, so I walked out of the agency and hid in the Walt Framer office for two years. Incidentally, not one single member of the Walt Framer staff ever made a disparaging remark about my white socks. Of course, some of the staff on "The Big Payoff" were lucky to *have* socks, so I'm not sure if I came out a winner.

My first Christmas party at the Brian Houston agency cost me twenty-two dollars. Two dollars for a necktie, and twenty dollars for a pair of shoes with laces. It was a complete waste of money, because the party had all the gaiety of a dentist's waiting room, and if it hadn't been for my boss, Bill Templeton, I would have vacated the premises immediately. Bill was the vice-president in charge of television, a three-fisted drinker, and the only man in the agency that talked to me.

Bill led me around for an hour, introducing me to all these agency guys who didn't want to meet me, and whom *I* didn't want to meet. At the end of the hour and nine straight bourbons, Bill was insulting these guys before *I* had a chance to insult them.

After our tenth straight bourbon, Bill introduced me to Brian Houston himself. This was *the* man. He had started the agency on a shoestring, and built the thing into a very respectable empire. He still owned the whole damn company, so what more can I say?

BILL:

> "Mr. Houston, this is Ken Whelan. . . . Mr. Whelan directs 'The Big Payoff,' the Colgate-Palmolive show."

HOUSTON:

> "Oh, yes. . . . Show business, right?"

ME:

> "I beg your pardon?"

HOUSTON:

> "Someone mentioned that you used to be in show business."

ME:

> "Well, yes. . . . Most television directors were in . . ."

HOUSTON:

> "Without being personal, I have to say that I've always resented the way you show people sneaked into the advertising business through the side door."

ME:

> "Without being personal, I have to say that I've always resented the way you advertising people sneaked into show business through the *back* door."

Terrific, uh? You can easily see why this little anecdote pops into my mind when someone mentions "The Big Payoff." I waited all my life for an insulting remark to which I would have the *perfect* answer. Mr. Houston gave me this wonderful moment, and I am grateful.

One year later, the Brian Houston agency held another Christmas party, and Mr. Houston gave me the only other anecdote that I remember about "The Big Payoff."

About midway in the party, the elevator doors opened, and Mr. Houston walked into a scene that was a little bit unusual. Remember, the party had been going on for more than two hours. The non-drinkers were feeling giddy from the cigarette smoke and the fumes of hundreds of martinis. The social drinkers were exposing themselves as holiday drunks. The alcoholics were stealing other people's drinks, or lying on the floor gasping for breath.

One of the social drinkers, a minor executive with the agency, was in the process of doing his version of the lampshade-on-the-head bit. He had found a plastic rubbish container, put it upside down over his head and then crouched down so that it covered his whole body. Then, he cut a peephole in the thing so he could see.

As Mr. Houston walked out of the elevator, this rubbish container came charging down the hall. It was really spooky, because you couldn't see the guy's feet moving inside the container. Through the peephole you could hear this guy yelling, "Make way for the tank! . . . Here comes the war tank! . . . Bang! Bang! Bang! . . . Boom! Boom! Boom! . . . Watch out for the tank! . . . Rat tat tat, rat tat tat! . . ."

As he passed Brian Houston, he rotated the container so that the peephole was facing the boss. A finger appeared through the peephole, like a gun barrel, "Rat tat tat! . . . *You're dead!*" Then, the container sped down the hallway and disappeared around a corner, with this crazy voice screaming, "Make way for the tank! . . . Here comes the tank!"

Mr. Houston turned to one of the big shots standing next to him, and said, "Fire that tank."

When someone mentions Perry Como, the instant image that pops into my mind is that of my own daughter. The incident happened a long time ago when Perry was doing a fifteen-minute live television show for CBS.

Every once in a while I would be assigned to the show as an associate director, and that's how Perry first noticed my daughter, or my daughter first noticed Perry . . . I'm not sure which way it was. My wife had brought Susan in town to watch the rehearsals, see the air show, and distract her father while he was trying to earn a living. At some time during the rehearsal period, Perry propositioned my daughter. Susan accepted the proposition with the full consent of her parents, because she was three years old.

Perry is a man of great taste who recognizes a true Irish beauty when he sees one. He wanted Susan to appear on his St. Patrick's Day show, and Susan thought the whole idea was great, because she had just fallen in love with Perry Como.

When the big day arrived, the rehearsals for Susan's musical number were smooth and professional. Perry Como, her assistant, remembered all the words of the song number, and Susan was brilliant.

The setting for the song number was a typical city scene, the steps of a brownstone house in the Bronx. Perry was supposed to sit on the steps and sing "Did Your Mother Come from Ireland." About sixteen bars into the song, Susan was supposed to walk in, sit on the steps beside Perry, and listen to him sing. Then there was a musical interlude while Perry picked Susan up, put her on his lap, and continued to sing the song to her.

As I said, the rehearsals were great. But, on the air show,

something happened that did not happen during rehearsal. At the risk of being a bore, I'm going to remind you that this was live television. . . . You couldn't correct the mistakes *or* accidents.

When we got on the air, everything went fine up to a certain point. Perry started the song, Susan walked in on time, the musical interlude was beautiful, and Susan ended up on Perry's lap without incident. . . .

As Perry started the second chorus of the song, the camera shot was a tight two-shot of Perry and Susan. Perry sang:

"Did your mother come from Ireland, did she . . ."

"Hic!"

The "hic" was from Susan. She was having an attack of the hiccups right in the middle of Perry's song, and in full view of millions of viewers. Perry stared at Susan as if he couldn't believe what was happening. He had lost his place in the song, but the orchestra leader was smart and went back to the beginning of the number.

"Did your mother come from Ireland, did she . . ."

"Hic!"

The studio audience had giggled at the first hiccup and now burst out laughing. Perry started to laugh, and for twenty seconds he just hugged Susan and laughed his head off.

Lee Cooly, the producer of the show, was standing offstage watching the whole thing. With all the earmarks of genius, he miraculously produced a glass of water.

Perry saw his producer waving the glass of water like a signal flag, and knew immediately what to do. He took Susan off his lap, sat her on the steps, stopped the orchestra, and said:

"We have a little problem here. . . . I think we should try to solve it before we continue the song."

For the next three minutes, Perry tried to get rid of Susan's hiccups. He told her to sip the water slowly while he counted to ten. They tried it four times before it worked. It was a *first* on network television—never before had three minutes of air time been devoted to the problem of hiccups.

When the hiccups were finally stopped, the audience applauded until their hands were red. When Perry finished singing the song to Susan, they gave him an ovation. Of course, the way the whole thing turned out, it was very smart show business, but I know it was much more than that. I think the incident revealed a large hunk of Perry's basic personality. For one thing, it certainly proved his reputation for being the most relaxed performer in show business. It took a very confident and relaxed man to react the way he did. But that's not all it revealed about Perry. I'm sure that there were other television stars who were secure enough and smart enough to react the same way, but it would have looked phony. It would have looked like a clever "piece of business," and the applause would have been for the star's quick thinking. The applause for Perry was not for his cleverness, it was for his sincere effort to get rid of a little girl's hiccups. I think he would have done the same thing for Susan with no one watching.

When someone mentions Dick Van Dyke in my presence, or if I see his name on the marquee of a movie theater, my mind immediately conjures up a picture of an alarm clock going off at two-thirty in the morning.

That alarm clock was my deadly enemy during the ten months I directed "The Morning Show" at CBS. At the time I directed it, the show starred Dick Van Dyke, with Merv Griffin and Sandy Stewart as vocalists and supporting personalities. Yes, it was *that* Merv Griffin.

The original star of "The Morning Show" was Jack Paar, but after a year of those terrible mornings, he finally begged off and was given a time slot at a more civilized hour. I don't know who first dubbed it "The Morning Show," but whoever he was, he had a very literal mind. We went on the air at seven in the morning, did a two-hour show for the East Coast, and then repeated one hour of the show for the West Coast. We had to be in the studio at five-thirty to talk everything over, check our signals, and possibly rehearse a couple of the song numbers. In order to get to the studio at five-thirty, most of us had to leave our suburban houses at four, or at the latest, four-thirty. To make sure that we left our suburban houses at four or four-thirty, we set our alarm clocks for three. I set *my* clock for *two-thirty,* because I was the director, very neurotic, and afraid that someone would beat me into the studio. Yes, there's no doubt about it. Whoever came up with the title, "The Morning Show," knew what he was talking about.

It just occurred to me that you are probably confused by my name dropping. Most people associate Jack Paar with the "Tonight" show at NBC, and you may have forgotten that he did "The Morning Show" at CBS, *before* he became famous. In fact, when you think about it, "The Morning Show" spawned Jack Paar, Dick Van Dyke, *and* Merv Griffin. Of course we didn't know that all three of them were destined to be television superstars during the sixties. Maybe it just proves out that old saying, "If you get up early in the morning, and apply your nose to the grindstone, you'll catch the worm and make tons of money." I think that's the way it goes.

After the alarm clock, the second image that pops into my mind when someone mentions Dick Van Dyke is a picture of Long Island's Southern State Highway at four o'clock in the morning during the worst rainstorm of the decade. Standing on the grass at the edge of the highway is a lonely figure, drenched to the skin. The figure is clutching a soggy attaché case to his chest, trying to keep it dry.

The forlorn figure was me. On that particular morning my

car had decided that it wasn't a submarine, and refused to start. At the time, I was living in Valley Stream, Long Island, and Dick Van Dyke was living in some crazy town that was twenty miles farther out on the Island. I called him and asked him to pick me up at the Valley Stream exit. I had never seen Dick Van Dyke's car, but on the phone he had told me to keep my eyes peeled for a blue Ford sedan.

So, when a blue Ford slowed down and stopped in front of me, there was no doubt in my mind that it was Dick Van Dyke.

When the car window rolled down, I stuck my head in and said, "Dick?"

It wasn't Dick. The driver was an extremely tan fat man wearing a knitted beret, four slave bracelets, and twelve rings.

"No, I'm Teddy," he said. "Does it make any difference?"

"Oh, I'm sorry, I'm waiting for Dick Van Dyke to pick me up. It's very nice of you to offer me a ride."

"Dick Van *Dyke!* . . . What a *fabulous* name. . . . It's absolutely campy. . . . You did say *Dyke,* didn't you?"

"Yes. . . . It *is* an unusual name, isn't it? . . . Thank you again for offering me a ride."

He adjusted his knitted beret in the rear-view mirror. "I think you're absolutely *fantastic.* I mean, it's four o'clock in the morning on Southern State Highway, in the middle of a cloud burst, and you're waiting for your friend to pick you up. . . . You must like him very much."

That did it. I was in no mood for humoring three-hundred-pound homosexuals. "Look, you fat faggot! I'm soaked to the skin, I think I'm coming down with pneumonia, and I'm very irritable! . . . So, why don't you haul your fruity ass out of here?"

"Bitch!"

He burned away one inch of his rear tires as he sped away. I had the feeling that he was kicking back at me with one of his high heels, and that he was aiming at my crotch.

Five minutes later, another blue Ford sedan stopped in front of me, and when the window rolled down I was extremely cautious about sticking my head into the car. I stood right where I was, on the edge of the highway, and shouted, "Dick Van Dyke?"

Dick's head appeared in the open car window. "No, I'm William Paley, but I'd be glad to drive you to Studio Forty-one if it will help CBS in any way."

"Very funny."

"For crying out loud, get in the car. . . . What's the matter with you?"

During the drive into the city I told Dick what had happened, and later on, while we were having coffee in the studio, I said to him, "Y'know, I learned something this morning. . . . There are a lot of civilians out there who are not in show business, and some of them are weird."

Years later, I realized that my remark was fairly profound. The very man I was talking to *was* in show business, and there wasn't a weird bone in his body. Dick was a straight, down-the-line family man, with a set of morals that would make the Pope turn green with envy. I always had the feeling that Dick would have been happier if he had been a Quaker missionary in China, *if* the Chinese didn't mind laughing once in a while.

Dick was one of the good ones, and in a business that is so heavily populated with psychotic kooks, it was a pleasure to work with a guy who was not a nut.

When I think about Merv Griffin back in those days, I remember him as a talented singer, and I also remember that he had a great potential talent as a *dancer*. That sounds crazy, doesn't it? I mean, if you are a fan of "The Merv Griffin Show," you know that Merv still sings a song once in a while, but I don't think you'll catch him trying to dance. Yet, the most fun I had on "The Morning Show" was trying to teach Merv a tap dance routine to go with one of his songs, or a few simple movements to spice things up. I don't know if Merv *wanted* to knock his brains out at six o'clock in the morning trying to be a dancer, but he knew I was an ex-dancer and choreographer, and I think he understood that I just couldn't be happy unless I had him prancing around while he was singing.

Of course, I was being ridiculous about the whole thing. It took two more years of directing before I realized that no one, absolutely *no one*, wanted to watch a song-and-dance man at seven o'clock in the morning. It took me seven more years of directing before I realized that most people would rather not look at *anything* at seven o'clock in the morning.

It's possible that Merv knew all this before I did, but he was a willing pupil, and by the time I left the show he was a pretty damn good hoofer.

If I had any brains I would have known that Merv was going to end up with his own show, and I could have stuck to him like glue, and today I would be a wealthy director or producer living in some glamorous place like Burbank, California. In fact, if I had any brains I would have known that Dick Van Dyke was going to end up making it big, and I could have stuck to him like glue, and today I would be the executive producer of all his movies and TV shows, and I'd have a luxurious home right in the middle of Disneyland.

Of course, I don't feel *too* guilty about not recognizing the big talents of Dick Van Dyke, Merv Griffin, or Jack Paar. There were a lot of executives at CBS who were just as dumb as I was. At the time I was directing "The Morning Show," all three of these gentlemen were owned by CBS, yet they all had to go to another network or another medium before their talents were showcased in the proper way. Think about it for a

"He could have made Gene Kelly tremble." (Merve Griffin and Judy Johnson on THE ROBERT Q. LEWIS SHOW. Same era as THE MORNING SHOW.)

moment. . . . On a certain Friday in the early fifties, Jack Paar stopped doing "The Morning Show." Two days later, on a Monday, Dick Van Dyke and Merv Griffin took over "The Morning Show." All of them ended up being fired or let go by CBS, and the three of them became the biggest stars of television during the sixties. Crazy, uh?

I mentioned TV executives in the last paragraph, which triggers another instant image. It has to do with a certain executive who was called "the hatchet man." This guy never worked for CBS as far as I know, but at one time or another he was on the staff of just about every local station in New York City. He was hired for one reason, and one reason only, and that was to put the fear of God into every single slave on the payroll. He seldom worked at any one station for more than a year, or possibly fifteen months, but during those fifteen months he made grown men weep, tough men beg, and lesser men grovel.

He was hired to play the bad guy, and he had a great talent for it. When a station decided that it was time to fire a lot of people, they sent for this boy. Sometimes the weeding out process was legitimate, sometimes it was just a cop-out for the general manager of the station who was looking for absolution. Whatever the reason, when the hatchet man had finished stacking up the bodies, the general manager and the other executives retained their good guy images, and the hatchet man moved on to another "contract."

Right now, in 1973, I can go to three local stations in New York City, look up a few old friends who have been working in the business for more than fifteen years, mention this guy's name, and watch their fingernails sweat.

By the end of the live television era, the hatchet man had perfected his blood bath techniques to a point that approached genius. His mass executions now had style and the touch of an artist. He hit his peak in 1959, when a certain local station hired him to do his thing.

Two days after he arrived on the scene, he ordered a meeting for the entire staff. The meeting was held in one of the TV studios, and when the victims arrived they were seated in bleachers that had been set up at one end of the studio. The hatchet man showed up twenty minutes later, and mounted a pulpit that had been left over from a religious show.

He started off by calling the roll. He hauled out a list of every member of the staff and their duties, and then the son of a bitch conducted the most deadly roll call since the Romans and the Christians.

"Alfred Wilson! . . . Just raise your hand and repeat your name!"

"Alfred Wilson! . . . Here!"

"Al, it says here that you're an associate producer in the news department. Is that true?"

"Yes. . . . That's . . . that's right."

"Al, are you married? . . . Do you support a family? . . . Children, things like that?"

"Well, yes. . . . I have two. . . ."

"That's wonderful, that really is wonderful. May I ask you another question. . . . Do you support this family by *trying* to be an associate producer in the news department?"

"Well, yes. . . . Of course. . . ."

"That's interesting . . . very interesting. . . ."

Then, the hatchet man would pick another name from his list. "Dan Cohen! . . . Do we have the honor of Dan Cohen's presence?"

"Here! . . . Dan Cohen, right here!"

"How old are you, Dan?"

"Twenty-four, sir . . . I'm twenty-four."

"Just a youngster, uh? . . . Tell me something, Dan. . . . Do you intend to make a career out of television?"

"Absolutely, sir. . . . Absolutely!"

The hatchet man's eyes went back to the list he held in his hand, then as an afterthought, he said, "Don't bet on it, Dan. . . . Don't bet on it." The eyes turned to the list again. "Peter Johnson! . . . Are we lucky enough to be blessed with Peter Johnson?"

"Right here! . . . In the back row, sir. . . . Peter Johnson!"

"I'm surprised to see you, Peter. . . . I didn't think you would show up. . . . I thought you might be sick."

"Sick? . . . No, I'm not sick. . . . I feel great."

"I'm glad to hear that, Peter, because I've got a little note written beside your name, and the note says that you had twenty-three sick days last year."

"Oh, that. . . . Yeah, I guess it was twenty-three days. . . . I had pneumonia."

"*And* you took your four weeks vacation, *and* you took off on all the Jewish holidays, *and* you're not even Jewish!"

"My wife is Jewish. . . . You see, I'm . . ."

"Mr. Johnson, *if* you are working for us *next* year, I suggest that you get pneumonia during your vacation period, and I also suggest that you make up your mind whether you are a Christian or a Jew!"

And so it went. Right down the list of seventy-six employees. When he had finished, he folded the list, put it into his pocket, and faced the trembling bleachers.

"Well, that's done with. . . . Thank you for being so patient. I know it was a tedious process, but I wanted to meet all of you face to face. . . . Now, I'd like to make an announcement. It's a very short announcement, so in case some of you have been bored by this meeting I can assure you that it will be all over in five minutes. . . . OK, here we go. This is the announcement: 'As of this moment, all of you are fired.' "

The trembling in the bleachers stopped. There was no need to tremble anymore. The axe had done its job.

The hatchet man continued:

"That's   right. . . . Every   single   one   of   you   is fired. . . . When you return to your offices, you will find a letter of dismissal signed by the general manager of this station, and me. . . . Right now, at this moment, *none* of you are working here!"

Stunned silence in the bleachers. A few independent souls started to leave, and one drunken Communist yelled, "Are you crazy or something? . . . You gotta be nuts! . . . I belong to a union!"

The hatchet man memorized this guy's face, and said, "Screw your union! . . . Now, if any of you people are interested, I'm going to talk for another half hour . . . explaining what you have to do to be rehired."

Deadly. . . . But, you have to admit that he had a touch of genius.

When someone mentions Percy Faith and his orchestra or Fay Bainter, I automatically think of Johnny Lincoln.

I doubt that I have to identify the first two names, but I don't expect you to know the third name. Johnny Lincoln was (and is) a cameraman at CBS. During the era of live television, when a good cameraman was worth his weight in gold, Johnny was worth his weight in diamonds. He also possessed a sense of humor that devastated quite a few directors.

The reason I connect Johnny Lincoln with Fay Bainter has to do with a Christmas show we did at CBS during the early fifties. The director was Fielder Cook, a very talented man who later distinguished himself by directing "Twelve Angry Men" and many other Golden Age classics.

The Christmas special was based on the story of Christ's birth. We had the Three Wise Men with camels, dozens of shepherds, two sheep, and a Jewish stable created by a scenic designer who was a Chinese faggot.

On this particular show Johnny Lincoln was assigned to the Houston crane camera, which was capable of lifting a camera and cameraman thirty feet above the studio floor. The camera was mounted on the end of a huge boom, and with the aid of an electric motor, plus five muscular technicians, the boom could move up and down like a giant cobra. The cameraman sat in a little bucket seat behind the camera, without a seat belt and without flight pay.

About halfway through the camera blocking rehearsal, the director told Johnny to boom up as high as he could go and get a shot of Fay Bainter right through the open roof of the stable. (I forget what part Fay was playing, but she was right there in the middle of the donkeys and the goats.) Johnny obeyed the director by going into orbit with his high flying camera, and ended up with the required shot.

The rehearsal continued for another hour and a half, but for some reason the director did not use Johnny's shot. Johnny just sat up there, patiently, and without uttering a word, for an hour and a half. The truth is that everyone in the control room forgot he was up there.

At the end of the camera blocking rehearsal we all broke for lunch. Everyone in the control room headed for the studio, where a table had been set up with coffee and sandwiches. As we walked into the studio we heard a voice from the sky.

"Hey, director, sir!" It was Johnny Lincoln's voice.

Fielder Cook looked up at the cameraman who was still perched thirty feet in the air, and gasped, "Oh my God, I forgot you were up there!"

Johnny scowled down at us, and said, "Can I ask you a question, Fielder? . . . What the hell am I supposed to be, the goddamn star of Bethlehem?"

I associate Percy Faith with Johnny Lincoln because of another classic one-liner from this witty cameraman, only this time *I* was the director—*and* the victim.

We were doing a closed-circuit show for Woolworth's, the five-and-ten people, and the show revolved around Percy Faith and his orchestra. (Just in case you don't know, a closed-circuit show never gets on the air. This particular show cost a hundred thousand dollars, and was piped to all the Woolworth folks scattered around the country. These five-and-ten people were forced to gather in auditoriums and offices for the sole purpose of listening to the Woolworth message. In between Percy's musical numbers, various executives from Woolworth's gave speeches that were designed to whip the organization into a frenzy of loyalty and financial success.)

We were in the middle of rehearsing Percy's big number, a medley of Rodgers and Hart songs, when I got this brilliant idea. I wanted a shot of Percy conducting the orchestra from the orchestra's point of view. In other words, I wanted to see Percy's face instead of the back of his head, and I wanted to see the studio audience in back of him. Now, this particular shot had been done hundreds of times before, but it took some

planning and forethought, because in order to pull it off you
needed a Houston crane or a hidden camera behind the orchestra. My planning and forethought had been a little delinquent,
but on the spur of the moment I decided to try it anyway.

I chose Johnny Lincoln to get the shot. Johnny was working over on the right side of the stage, shooting across at the violin and cello sections. At one point in the Rodgers and Hart
medley, the violin section had a rather long passage that lasted
about a minute and a half, so I planned to use camera two for
this violin stuff while I sneaked Johnny back against the brass
and the woodwinds to get the shot I wanted. . . . Incidentally,
it is very important for you to know that I was operating out of
a blind control room, with no big glass window through which I
could see the entire stage. The only clues I had were what the
camera monitors showed me.

The first time we tried to rehearse the shot, I told Johnny
to back up to the brass section and we'd try it from there. It
was no good.

"You're too close to Percy, Johnny. . . . Pull back some
more."

Johnny's voice came over my head set. "OK, hold it up a
minute. I'll ask a couple of these clarinet players to move their
chairs out of the way."

The second time we tried it he was still too close to Percy.

"No good, Johnny. . . . You gotta pull back at least three
more feet."

Johnny's voice again, a trifle more irritated: "All right, all
right. . . . I'll talk to the trumpet players, maybe they can let
me in a little farther."

The third time we rehearsed the sequence, it still didn't
work.

"No good, Johnny. . . . Go back another three feet."

I expected some of Johnny's creative profanity to come

pouring through my head set, but all I heard was complete silence.

"Johnny, can you hear me?"

More silence throuth the head set.

"Hey, Johnny! Talk to me, will ya! . . . Don't get all pissed off about it, just talk to me."

More silence.

"Johnny, all we need is three more feet! . . . Just pull back three feet!"

As I waited for an answer, I felt someone tap me on the shoulder. I turned my head to see who it was, and looked into the glaring eyes of Johnny Lincoln. He leaned closer to me, and yelled, "I *can't* pull back three more feet! . . . I'm up to my ass in bassoons!"

CHAPTER 15

The
Stillbirth
of a
Golden Age
Television Show

A few years ago, Merle Miller and another guy whose name I can't remember wrote a very funny book called "Only You, Dick Daring!" Merle and this other fellow were (and are) a couple of pro writers who in a moment of weakness agreed to write the pilot script for a television series. In the book they told about their experiences in making this pilot show. One of the funniest scenes in the book was a creative session with Jim Aubrey, who at the time was head of programming for CBS. If the reader was close to the business of television, and had come in contact with TV executives, he probably found the incident funny and *believable.* If the reader was one of those fortunate civilians who made an honest living, and had never dealt with TV executives, he probably thought that the chapter was funny but *unbelievable.*

Believe *me,* as someone who toiled in the vineyards of live television for many years, that creative session with Jim Aubrey was absolutely believable.

I've sat in on the rape, which started the pregnancy, which ended in the birth of many a television show. During some of these creative sessions, I listened to TV executives who made Jim Aubrey sound like Shakespeare at his most creative moment.

Let me tell you about one of these sessions that ended in the "stillbirth" of a TV show.

It all started with a creative meeting which was held in this particular executive's office on the fourteenth floor of 485 Madison Avenue. I had been assigned to direct the pilot of a new show, and was told to show up at this creative meeting. I knew absolutely nothing about the show. I didn't know if it was a musical show, a situation comedy, a panel show, or a kids' show. As I was going up in the elevator to the fourteenth floor, it occurred to me that the elevator operator probably knew more about it than I did.

When I walked into the office I was greeted by one of our top ranking Rabbit-Hole fellows. (I'm going to call him Jim, although that isn't his real name. In fact, I'm not going to use real names. I wish I could say that my reluctance to identify these people was a noble streak in me, but the fact is, I just might end up working with some of them again, and it would be awkward.)

Anyway, Jim the rabbit guy greeted me with, "Glad to have you aboard, Ken. . . . Been hearing a lot of good things about you." His handshake said something like, "I got stuck with you. . . . I didn't have anything to say about it, and you certainly don't *look* like a good director."

Jim introduced me to the various people scattered around the office.

"Ken, this is Mark . . . and Leo. . . . They'll be writing the show for us. Fellas, this is Ken, our director."

I started to shake hands with them. "Nice to meet you, I . . ." They stared at my hand as if I were holding a knife, and then nodded their heads to let me know that they had been officially introduced. I knew immediately that they weren't *real* writers, because writers don't act that way when they're introduced to other people in the business. Writers are very lonely. They do their work alone, which is the only way it can be done, and when they come out of hiding to present their work, they usually get clobbered to death by second guessers. Writers need *friends,* especially if the friends could be the director or producer of what they had written. When a *real* writer is introduced to the man who will be directing his work, he grasps the director's hand with *both* of his hands, and smiles a lot. It's more of a pleading gesture than a friendly gesture. What the writer is saying is, "Please don't ruin what I have written! . . . I've worked for a long time on it, and I think it's pretty good. . . . I gave birth to it. . . . It's my baby! . . . For God's sake, don't screw it up!"

That's why I knew that Mark and Leo weren't real writers. I knew they had never written anything, and that they never *would* write anything. I guessed that they were former carnival men who had worked their way up the midway until they finally got to television.

"Ken, this is Mike Conners . . . your producer." Jim pointed in the direction of a short guy with glasses who blinked at me a couple of times.

"Mike has been doing *big* things in Denver, so we brought him in to the *big* time." Jim said that.

I said, "Big things in *Denver?*"

"Colorado," said Jim. "Denver, Colorado."

"Oh, sure."

Jim walked over to the leather sofa which dominated one wall of the office, and I followed him. A big fat guy was stretched out on the sofa looking like he was sound asleep. He was wearing green slacks, a brown sport jacket, basketball sneakers, and a toupee that looked like dyed sauerkraut. A cigar protruded from one of the many folds of flesh underneath his nose.

Jim introduced me to the sleeping fat guy. This is Jerome Dietrich. . . . He's our developer. He's from the Coast."

"What's a developer?" I asked.

The fat guy's cigar jiggled a couple of times, and he talked. "This is a wise guy, Jim. . . . I don't even have to open my eyes, and I know he's a wise guy."

I was embarrassed. "Oh, I'm sorry. . . . I didn't know you were awake. . . ."

Jim suddenly forgot my first name. "Whelan, you're starting off on the wrong foot. . . . Now, let's get with it, uh?"

"I'm sorry. . . . I wasn't trying to be a wise guy. It's just that I've never worked with a developer before."

Jim ignored me, and walked to his desk. He selected a pipe from his pipe rack, filled it with tobacco, and then spent two or three minutes getting the pipe lit. From behind a cloud of pipe smoke he stared at us for another thirty seconds. The room was vibrating with anticipation as we waited for him to speak. (Except for Jerome, the developer, who looked like he had fallen asleep again.)

Finally, Jim spoke. "For God's sake, Whelan . . . sit down! . . . What are you going to do, stand up for the whole meeting?"

I sat down while Jim walked slowly to the double window behind his desk. He stood there for a moment, staring out the window, and puffing on his pipe. It was like a scene out of an old Ronald Colman movie, where Ronald is about to tell his officers that they have to attack the Arab hordes at dawn. I had a strong feeling that I knew what Jim was going to say.

Jim continued to look out the window as he said, "Gentlemen, I am looking out over a city. A great city. The city of New York . . ."

One of the writers scribbled something in his notebook, which made me a little curious. I mean, the writer *did* have the look of a heavy drinker, but he *must* have known he was in New York. The producer cleaned his glasses and tried to focus his eyes on the ceiling. The developer's cigar fell out of his mouth, and he stopped snoring. Personally, I was impressed with Jim's opening statement, but it only strengthened my strong feeling. I *knew* what Jim was going to say.

Jim continued, still gazing out at the skyline. "Gentlemen, do you know what this city is full of?"

I had an answer, but I controlled myself and kept my mouth shut.

Jim turned away from the window and stared at us for a moment. Then he answered his own question. "This city is full of *people!*"

The producer said, "I see what you mean, Jim."

Both writers scribbled something in their notebooks.

I couldn't think of a suitable reaction, so I suddenly discovered a loose button on my jacket, and it became terribly important. You see, I *knew* what Jim was going to say next, because I had seen this act before. It was listed as "approach number three" in the executive handbook.

Jim was staring out the window again. "Yes, this city is filled with people. These people watch television . . ." He turned to us again. "Right?"

I found myself saying, "I hope to God they do!"

"Good point," said the producer.

The developer's cigar fell off his shirt front, and started to burn a hole in the rug.

Jim returned to the window. "The United States of America is filled with cities like this. These cities are filled with people who watch television . . . correct?"

Now, I knew I was right. Jim *was* doing "approach number three" in the executive handbook, no doubt about it. This particular approach was a favorite with executives who really didn't have a *concrete idea* for a new show. When the poor bastards couldn't think of a new idea for a show, they would gather together a few flunkies, hold a creative session, and go into their act.

I always imagined that there was a basic script for "approach number three" and it went something like this. All the executive had to do was memorize it.

Management Directive—No. 34-A
Subject: Approach No. 3—(To All Execs)

STAGE DIRECTION:

(At first opportunity, walk to window, and gaze out across New York City. Repeat the following dialogue word for word.) "Gentlemen, we are about to embark on a great adventure. . . . I have hand-picked each and every one of you. The fact that you're sitting in this office is a tacit tribute to your talent and creative ability."

ADVICE TO EXECUTIVE:

(If the flunkies applaud the above statement, they are phonies, and should not be trusted. If the flunkies make rude noises with their mouths, they are communist militants, and should not be trusted. If the flunkies remain silent and exchange knowing looks, you have the right kind of flunkies. They *know* you are talking pure bullshit, but they're willing to go along with it. . . . Make decision about flunkies, and proceed with following dialogue.) "Yes, gentlemen, we lucky few have been chosen to participate in the creation of the most exciting, the most relevant, and the most original show that has ever been seen on television."

STAGE DIRECTION:

(At this point, open the window, so that the noise of the city can be heard by the flunkies. Continue gazing out window.) "There are people out there, gentlemen. Beautiful people, ugly people, rich people, poor people . . . Some of these people are Republicans, some of them are Democrats, and some of them just don't vote. But, they're *all* people! . . . Right, gentlemen?"

ADVICE TO EXECUTIVE:

(Do not expect a reaction to this statement. If you have the right flunkies, they won't want to embarrass you.) "These wonderful people pay our salaries, gentlemen. . . . And *they* own the airways! . . . Think about that for a moment."

STAGE DIRECTION:

(For the next hunk of dialogue, you will *have* to make an on-the-spot decision. If the show is a *local* show, gaze down at Madison Avenue, and refer to the people in the street below you. . . . If the show is a *network show,* fix your eyes on the top of the Empire State Building, as if you were looking across the whole country. . . . If you are an imaginative executive, and can make believe that William Paley is sitting on top of the Empire State Building, it will help a lot.) "Gentlemen, we *owe* something to these people! . . . We are in their debt, and they must be paid! . . . Is there one person in this office who does not feel this responsibility?"

STAGE DIRECTION:

(A dramatic pause is effective at this moment. Leave William Paley sitting on top of the Empire State Building, turn, and fix your gaze on the flunkies.) "Well?"

ADVICE TO EXECUTIVE:

(At this moment, your flunkies will be leafing through old copies of *Life* magazine, reading match book covers, or working cross-word puzzles. . . . Do *not* be discouraged, and continue with the following dialogue.) "Yes, guys, we do owe them something, and we're going to pay them back. . . . We're going to give these wonderful people *their own* show! . . . A show dedicated to *their* interests, *their* problems, *their* lives!"

STAGE DIRECTION:

(Bow your head, and stare at your shoes. Try to feel humble. . . . If you wear glasses, remove glasses before bowing head.) "Guys, are you with me? . . . Do you understand what I'm trying to say?" (Walk to window, put your glasses back on, and stare out at city again. Remember, stare down at the street if it's a local show, and fix your eyes on the top of the Empire State Building if it's a network show. If you could visualize William Paley *and* Frank Stanton sitting on top of the Empire State Building, it might be a plus, because in the next five minutes you're going to need all the inspiration you can muster. Continue dialogue.) "Yes, guys. . . . This is going to be an exciting, dynamic, meaningful show . . . created *for* the people, *by* the people, and dedicated to the proposition that all people, have an equal share in the airways. . . . Well, gentlemen, that's about it. I know that I have picked the right team, and I know that you're with me all the way. . . . Good luck, and God bless you."

ADVICE TO EXECUTIVE:

(One of your flunkies may be single and without family obligations. This type of flunky seems to shy away from ass-kissing, and should be kicked off the team *before* the big game. These radicals usually expose themselves at moments like this. You can spot them right away, because they always ask crazy questions, like, "It sounds fine, but what is the idea behind the show? . . . What is the show going to be *about*?" If you run into this kind of nonsense, make a mental note to have this guy turn in his stopwatch the following morning, and continue with the following dialogue.) "Obviously, you haven't been listening to what I've been saying. . . . This show is going to be about those people out there!. . . . Every one of those people have a story locked up inside them. . . ."

STAGE DIRECTION:

(Stare down at Madison Avenue) ". . . For instance, right now I'm looking at a bus, stopping at a bus stop on the street below me. . . . Our first twenty shows could be based on the first twenty people who step off *that bus*! . . . Right?"

ADVICE TO EXECUTIVE:

(This last statement should wrap up the meeting. Dismiss the flunkies, close the window, and go to a well-deserved three-hour lunch.)

P.S. TO EXECUTIVE:

(In some instances, the non-ass-kissing bachelor may have self-destructive tendencies. Of course, the poor fellow doesn't *know* that he has this drive toward failure, but in reality, his subconscious is not happy in big-time television, and would feel much more comfortable at a small station in Alaska. In cases like this, the unfortunate soul will find himself asking questions like, "Wait a minute! . . . Isn't that a rather vague idea for a television show? . . . I mean, what's the premise of the show? What's the format? . . . It seems to me that I've heard that 'first twenty people off the bus' routine before.")

STAGE DIRECTION:

(Pause thirty full seconds before responding to this sick question. *Do not* look at the neurotic guy who asked the question. Use the thirty seconds to study the reactions of the other members of the team. If they look shocked at this weird question, or if they wink at you, then you have the right team, minus one. If one of the good guys chokes on his coffee when he hears this question, make *him* the producer. . . . End the meeting with the following dialogue.) "I'm going to ignore the last question, because I wish to end this meeting with a feeling of 'gung ho' and 'go get 'em.' I think this show can be a winner, and as I pass the baton to you guys, I can only say, 'go get 'em! . . . And 'gung ho,' too.'")

P.S. TO EXECUTIVE:

(Don't forget to bounce the mental-case guy off the show. Do not feel guilty about this action, because you are actually doing him a favor. His dismissal from the show is simply the first leg of his long journey to that small station in Alaska, where his subconscious will be happy and content. Take a four-hour lunch. You deserve it.)

THE END

To get back to Jim, I watched him do the window routine for a few more minutes, and then I realized that something was wrong. Jim wasn't sticking to the script. He stopped doing "approach number three" and started to use his own words. He was still staring at the top of the Empire State Building, but the dialogue sounded strange.

"Gentlemen, I want to ask you a question." He turned toward us, picked up a pipe cleaner from the top of his desk, and cleaned his pipe. Two minutes later, he said, "Gentlemen, those people out there are very much like you and me. . . . I think you'll all agree with that. . . . Now, here's the question. . . . What is the *one* thing that you and I have always been a sucker for? From the time we were little children, right through our adult lives, what is *one* thing that has always been intriguing and fascinating?"

He lit his pipe again, which gave us a minute to think. Then, from behind his usual cloud of smoke, he said, "Well?"

"Broads," said one of the writers.

Jim waved the smoke away from him so that he could give this unfortunate writer the evil eye. "You found 'broads' intriguing when you were *six years old?*"

"It was an impulsive answer, Jim. . . . I'll do better after I've warmed up." The writer avoided Jim's gaze, and started to jot things down in his notebook. (He probably jotted down something like, "Screw you, Jim.")

"Music," said the producer-type guy. "Music has always been the most fascinating thing in my life. . . . It all began . . ."

"Well, at least that's a sensible answer, Leonard. It's not the right answer, but it's a sensible answer."

"It all began when I was six years old," said Leonard. "I was listening to the Boston Pops Orchestra on the radio, and suddenly they started to play Ravel's *Bolero* . . ."

"That's beautiful," said Jim. "It's not only beautiful, it's intelligent. However, this is not going to be a musical show. I'm talking about . . ."

Leonard continued. ". . . Right now, at the age of forty-five, when I hear Ravel's *Bolero*, I get goose pimples. . . . Just the other night, I . . ."

"Knock it off, Leonard!" said Jim. "Music is not the right answer. I'm thinking of a subject that has *universal* appeal. From childhood, right through to old age, this subject is catnip to *everybody!* . . . Well?"

Jim looked over at the developer guy who was stretched out on the leather sofa. The fat fellow was obviously faking his cat nap, because when Jim looked in his direction, he snorted a couple of times, and rolled over to face the wall. I figured that he didn't want any part of this guessing game.

Jim looked at me. "Whelan?"

"Money," I said. "Money is the most universal subject in the world."

"That's a very good answer, Whelan," said Jim.

"Thank you," I said.

"I'm surprised," said Jim.

"I withdraw the thank you," I said.

"There you go again, Whelan. One minute you make a great deal of sense, and the next minute you're being a wiseass!" He returned to the window, and resumed his man-of-destiny attitude. When he looked out that window, I really believed that he could see every single person in the United States. He lowered his voice to a dramatic whisper, and said, "Gentlemen, we're going to do a *magic* show. . . ."

"A what?" I asked, in my usual wiseass tone of voice.

"Of course," said the producer. "I should have known. Magic is indeed the most universal subject in the world. From childhood through old age, magic is the one thing that fascinates every human being. . . . I remember when I was six years old, and my mother took me to see . . ."

"Knock it off, Leonard," said Jim. *"I'm* running this creative session."

The writers stopped making notes, and one of them said, "A magic show? . . . umph . . . Sounds OK to me."

"Deal *me* in," said the other writer.

The developer suddenly became wide awake, and sat up on the sofa like a walrus claiming his favorite ice floe. "A magic show, uh? . . . I think you've got something there, Jim. . . . Now, let's develop it."

"There's just one question I'd like to ask," said one of the writers.

"Fire away," said Jim. "That's what this meeting is all about. I'm trying to create a climate that encourages questions and answers, and a freedom to create."

"Well," said the writer. "Well, now you might think that this is a dumb question, but . . ."

"There is no such thing as a dumb question in this office," said Jim. "A creative climate is what I'm after. . . . Fire away!"

"Well," said the writer, "what do writers *write* on a magic show?"

Like an idiot, I had to open my big mouth. "Oh, they write things like 'abracadabra,' and 'presto' . . . things like that."

"That's *enough*, Whelan! . . . Just sit there and listen. Maybe you'll learn something."

Jim walked back to the window, lit his pipe again, and took a deep breath. "Gentlemen, let me try to communicate a few of the ideas I have about this show. . . . Now, as I've said before, magic is something that appeals to *everyone*. But the fact that we have a universal subject *doesn't* guarantee that we'll have a hit show." Jim walked back to his desk, put down his pipe, and took a quick peek at some notes he had written on the back of an envelope. "To prove my point, let's talk about religion for a moment. . . . I think you'll agree with me when I say that religion is a universal subject."

We all nodded our heads in agreement.

The developer said, "Can't argue with you on that statement. Religion is very big on the Coast."

"Of course it is," said Jim. "Yet, the fact that religion is a universal subject does not guarantee its acceptance by one hundred percent of the market. . . . Think about that for a moment."

We thought about it for a moment.

"You see what I mean, gentlemen?" said Jim. "Even though religion is one of the most universal subjects in the world, there's an awful lot of atheists walking around."

"Good point," said the developer.

One of the writers said, "Would you repeat that last part? I'd like to write it down."

Jim continued. "Do you know *why* religion doesn't accomplish one hundred percent saturation of the market? . . . It's the way they *present* it, gentlemen. . . . The key word is *presentation!*"

I found myself saying, "I'll go along with *that*. . . . I'm a Catholic, and I've always wanted to direct a new version of eleven o'clock Mass."

Jim stared at me a moment, trying to figure out if I was being a wiseass again, made his decision, and continued. "This show will live or die on the way we handle the subject of magic. . . . For instance, I do not want a *children's* magic show. It should appeal to children, of course, but, I want this to be an *adult* magic show. . . . On the other hand, I don't want a magic show that is *too* adult. I mean, I don't want a pseudo-intellectual show that only appeals to the eggheads in the cosmopolitan areas. . . . Of course, it must have *some* appeal for the eggheads, but it must also hit the farmer in Nebraska right in his breadbasket. . . . The show must have something for our Jewish audience, our Polish audience, our rich audience, and our poor audience. And, gentlemen, let's not forget the huge segment of our potential audience who are Negro. My God, with *their* background *this* show should get one hundred percent Negro saturation. . . . You know what I mean?"

"Good point," said the developer. "Their whole culture is based on witch doctors, magic potions, voodoo, and that sort of stuff. . . . Very good thinking, Jim. . . . This show will hit these people right in their hominy grits."

The writers and the producer made various noises that indicated approval of these statements. I couldn't believe what I was hearing, so I shut my mouth, and made believe that the ceiling of Jim's office was fascinating.

"What about you, Whelan?" asked Jim. "I notice that you're staring at the ceiling in a very negative manner. . . . Are you with us, or against us? . . . Are you ready to direct the greatest magic show that's ever been done? And, what's more important, do you *believe* in our magic show?"

"I'm ready! I'm ready!" I answered. "And I believe in the show, I really do." . . . (I was deadly serious about this next statement.) . . . "I think that magic is a fascinating subject, and I think we have a great opportunity to fill one hour of television time with the best magic show that has ever been seen. . . . It's . . ."

Jim interrupted me. "That's nice, Whelan. . . . But . . ."

"It's an exciting idea! . . . We can assemble the three greatest magicians in the world, and we can present them in a one-hour special that will knock the public right on their asses. . . . I really believe in this show, and I'm going to do everything I can to make this magic show a winner!"

Jim tried to interrupt again. "That's *very* nice, Whelan. . . . But, I'm afraid that you . . ."

"I think a one-hour special on the subject of magic is a brilliant idea." I was really sincere about this whole thing, and I was rising to the occasion. "I'm sure that we can do a magic show that is exciting and important! . . . If we're successful, we can do a magic show every year, like the Christmas shows, and the Oscar Awards."

Jim stared at me for a long time. "Whelan, what the hell are you talking about? . . . This is going to be a *weekly* show. . . . We're going to do a magic show *every week*. . . . At nine-thirty, on Monday nights."

"You're kidding," I said.

Jim stared at me for a *long, long* time. "Whelan, I pegged

you as a negative person the moment you walked through the door. . . . I have been patient with you, but. . ."

"Three great magicians *every week?*" I knew I was saying the wrong things, but I couldn't stop. "We're going to need three topnotch magicians every seven days? Is that what you're saying?"

Jim gave me a look of disgust, then he walked back to the window in a very military manner. I watched him stare out the window, and I knew he was trying to remember the script of "Approach No. 3." He tried to light his pipe, but his anger kept blowing the match out, so he ended up with a pipe that was as cold as his heart. "Whelan, I've had just about enough out of you!" . . . He kept looking out the window. "I've tried to establish a creative climate at this meeting! . . . A positive, affirmative, creative climate. . . . But all I've heard from you is negative bullshit, and wisecracks! . . . Now, I'm . . ."

"But, there're only ten or eleven professional magicians in show business! We'll run out of magicians in a month. . . . Then what do we do?"

I heard a strange snapping noise, and I saw the bowl of Jim's pipe fall to the floor. He had bitten through the stem of his pipe in sheer fury.

"There you go again, Whelan! Negative bullshit!" He removed the remains of the pipe from his mouth. "You're not a creative person, Whelan. . . . Let's face it. You're not a positive, affirmative person. . . . You're negative! You just aren't a creative human being! . . . And, I don't want to hear . . ."

"But . . ."

"I don't want to hear another word out of you for the rest of the meeting. . . . Is that understood? . . . Not one single word."

I looked at the pipe bowl lying on the carpet, and realized he was deadly serious. So I shut up.

The next half hour of Jim's creative session was spent discussing the really important things in TV production. Jim
thought that the tickets for the studio audience should be blue.
("Blue is the color of magic," he said.) The developer from the
Coast suggested that the cameramen wear white ties and tail
coats, *and* tall silk opera hats. ("In keeping with the theme of
our show," he explained.) One of the writers wanted to discuss
the office he was going to work in. He claimed that he couldn't
write a word if his office wasn't decorated by his
mother. . . . The other writer wanted to know the name and
address of every Chinese restaurant within ten blocks of the
CBS building. ("I can only eat food that digests fast," he said.
"Trouble in the lower colon, y'know?") The producer spent ten
minutes discussing the credits for the end of the show. He
wanted to make sure that his name would be in bigger letters
than the director's name. ("But, not as big as *your* name,
Jim," he assured.)

Once they got through discussing this really important
stuff, they got down to the actual show. Jim thought that the
first thing they should kick around was the opening of the
show. ("The station break is over," he said. "They cut to our
studio. . . . We come up on a camera shot. . . . Now, what
do we see? . . . That's what I'm tossing at you, gentlemen. . . . What do we see?")

Sounds crazy, doesn't it? They spent the next hour dreaming up ways to open the show, *before* they discussed the format
of the show, talent possibilities, or anything else that was *really* important.

During that hour, I heard one of the writers suggest that
the host for the show should be dressed like Merlin the magician, and that he should appear through a trap door in the
stage floor. . . . .The producer came up with a beauty. He
thought the show should open with a camera shot of a huge

gong. ("About twenty feet in diameter," he said.) He then went on to visualize six beautiful chorus girls holding a ten-foot mallet. ("We come up on the shot of the gong. . . . The girls come dancing in with the mallet. . . . The girls give the gong a bang with the mallet, and the show begins!") The developer from the Coast thought that the show should open in the street outside the studio. He wanted to put a straitjacket on the show's host, hang him by his heels from the top of the building, and have the guy introduce the show upside down.

I listened to their creative ideas for a full sixty minutes without opening my mouth. I heard things that you wouldn't believe. The three suggestions I mentioned were the *best* ideas I heard during the entire hour.

Finally, my mind snapped, and I joined the insanity.

I had an idea.

"What about this, fellas?" I said. "What if . . ."

Jim turned on me like a divorced wife. "Whelan, I warned you! . . . You're not a creative human being . . . you're negative."

"That was an hour ago," I answered. "I'm positive now. . . . Honest to God, I'm positive!"

Jim sighed and walked to the window. There was a long pause as he changed into Clive of India. "Very well, Whelan. . . . I would never want it to be said that I discouraged creative thought. . . . Speak."

"What if we opened on a tight shot of a magician's hand? . . . He's wearing a white glove, and the background is black." I started to get excited about the idea, so I stood up and started to demonstrate. "The white-gloved hand is producing cards out of thin air. . . . An ace of diamonds appears from nowhere . . . then a ten of clubs seems to jump into his hand. . . . We cue the orchestra, and suddenly he is holding a plain white card with the show's title printed on it. . . . The music hits a crescendo, and the jack of hearts pops into his hand. . . . As the music hits its high point, we do a matched dissolve to another camera, and the host of the show seems to walk right through the jack of hearts and into the living room of our home viewer!''

There was a long silence, which baffled me. I thought the idea was brilliant, and I had anticipated a round of applause, or at least a bravo or two.

"Well?" I pleaded. "What do you think?"

"It's an old idea, Whelan," said one of the writers.

"Yeah," said the other writer. "It sounds kind of familiar. . . . I think they did that in a Fu Manchu movie."

The producer studied the look on Jim's face, trying to read his boss's reaction. Then he said, "Well, for all intents and purposes, it *could* be a good idea. . . . But, on the other hand, it may be a little contrived. . . . What do you think, Jim?" Jim?"

"It's not bad, Whelan, not bad at all." Then Jim smiled at me. It was the same kind of smile that the Pope bestows on people who have just kissed his ring.

"It's not exactly my cup of tea," continued Jim. "But, it's a good try, Whelan. At least it's not negative. . . . Now, let's put on our creative hats and see if we can come up with something that has some class."

The developer from the Coast did not bother to voice his opinion about my idea, but I noticed that he was smoking his cigar in a negative manner.

The creative session continued for another half hour, as they searched for an idea that met with Jim's approval. Finally, they ran out of gas. There were long pauses between suggestions, and the ideas had disintegrated into childish nonsense.

During one of the long pauses, the walrus guy from the Coast struggled off the sofa and onto his feet. It occurred to me that he looked much better when he was horizontal.

He took the cigar out of his mouth.

"Jim," he said. "I think we passed up the diamond without knowing it. . . . In the last hour and a half we've come up with a lot of zircons . . . good zircons, and bad zircons . . . big zircons, and little zircons. . . . But, among all these zircons there was *one* diamond . . . and, we missed it!"

"That's an exciting statement," said Jim.

The walrus guy continued. "Jim, about a half hour ago, *you* had an idea that was rejected by us fellows. I think if we had kicked it around a little more we would have realized it was a diamond. . . . But, we rushed by it, and underestimated the sparkle of a true gem."

"What idea was that?" said Jim. "I mean, I've come up with *so many* ideas in the last hour and a half . . ."

The pro from the Coast took a dramatic puff from his cigar. "If I remember correctly, you suggested that we open the show with a tight shot of a magician's hand. . . . You said that the hand should be clothed in a white glove, and that the background should be black . . ."

"Oh sure," said Jim. "I remember that one."

". . . then you said that the hand produces a playing card out of thin air. . . . I hope that I'm quoting you correctly."

"Absolutely," said Jim. "You're on the nose!"

The fat man picked up his cue like a pro. "I don't remember the nitty gritty of the idea, but I think you said that the hand ends up with the jack of hearts, and then we'd do a matched dissolve to another camera . . ."

Jim finished the statement. "Right, the host would appear to walk through the jack of hearts."

I was stunned. I think I started to blubber.

"That's the diamond, Jim," said the Coast guy.

"Of course," said Jim. "How could we have missed it?"

The walrus fellow flopped back on the sofa as if he was taking a bow. "I'd just like to make one little change . . . if you don't mind, Jim."

"Be my guest," said Jim. "*You're* the developer."

"Instead of a white glove against a black background . . . I think it should be a black glove against a white background."

"Absolutely perfect," said Jim. "Just the right touch."

The fat guy put the cigar back in his mouth, closed his eyes, and smiled.

I thought I was going to throw up, so I started for the door.

Jim closed the meeting. "Well, fellows . . . you've got your opening! Now go out there, and bring me back a show!"

Five minutes later I stumbled out of 485 Madison Avenue in a state of shock, and I stayed that way for seven more years of live television.

P.S.   I was fired off the show two days later.

P.P.S.   The show never ran short of magicians, because it was taken off the air after one performance.

CHAPTER **16**

If It
Ever Happens
Again,
I'll Skip It

In many ways, the Golden Age of Television was not as Golden as you might remember. The live dramatic shows that are now discussed with a reverence due only to Shakespeare were often just a step higher than an amateur performance. Thousands of dramatic shows were produced during the era of live television, and very few of them were really good. Older folk, like myself, are always saying things like, "Those were days when they did *real* dramatic shows! . . . My God, the taped junk they put on the air *these* days can't compare to the old live shows."

When you hear someone make a remark like that, forgive them, because they are remembering a few great, classic shows

209

like "Marty," "Twelve Angry Men," or maybe an exceptional show on "Studio One." Time makes a liar out of the past, especially in show business. The golden part of the live television era consisted of a few special people who had a lot of talent. The rest of it was rather ordinary.

Sid Caesar was one of those special people who had more talent than the industry deserved. It is very possible that Sid Caesar was (and is) the greatest comedy actor and pantomimist that ever lived. Sure, I know all about Chaplin, Buster Keaton, Jean Louis Barrault, Marcel Marceau, etc. . . . and I still think that Sid Caesar was (and is) more talented than any of them. If his name doesn't go down in show business history as being one of the greatest, it will be because he picked live television as his medium. As someone once said about radio, live television was like "writing on a cake of ice." Once the show was over, it melted away, leaving a smooth cake of ice and nothing for posterity. The only records of Sid Caesar's greatness are a few beat-up kinescopes that look as if someone spilled coffee on them.

Sid's writers were some of the special people who sprinkled a lot of gold dust on live television. I'll drop a couple of names, and you'll see what I mean. . . . Neil Simon, Mel Brooks, Carl Reiner, and I *think* Woody Allen wrote for the show. Since they're all millionaires by now, I believe it's safe to say that they were a golden group.

There were a few brilliant producers who did their best to lift early television out of its mediocre pattern. Fred Coe was one of them, Max Liebman was another, and of course, Worthington Miner. (There were a couple of other good producers, but these three were my favorites and are sufficient to make my point.)

For every Fred Coe there were twenty dramatic show producers who couldn't produce a match. For every Max Liebman there were twenty musical show producers who thought that a libretto was a musical instrument. For every Worthington Miner there were twenty producers who had never even seen a Broadway play.

There were five or six directors who had the golden touch.

"He paved the way with STUDIO ONE."

I've mentioned their names before, and I'm going to mention them again. For my money, the big ones were Franklin Schaffner, Fiedler Cook, Arthur Penn, Ralph Nelson, Marty Ritt, John Frankenheimer, and Sidney Lumet. I'm sure that there were a couple of other good ones that escape my memory, but these are the guys who were the backbone of live television. They were my heroes, and for every one of them there were twenty other directors who couldn't direct traffic on a one-way street.

Yes, there were several pure nuggets that created the myth of the Golden Age, but most of live television was just plain brass.

It was a growing period. An era that had to be lived through, in order to get to something that was better. . . . And it *is* better these days, believe me, and it will get better every year that it exists.

The age of live television has been dead for fourteen years. It is over and done with, and it will never return. . . . Thank God!